AFRICAN AMERICAN LEGISLATORS
IN THE AMERICAN STATES

Power, Conflict, and Democracy:
American Politics Into the 21st Century
Robert Y. Shapiro, Editor

D1275083

Power, Conflict, and Democracy:
American Politics Into the Twenty-first Century
Robert Y. Shapiro, Editor

This series focuses on how the will of the people and the public interest are promoted, encouraged, or thwarted. It aims to question not only the direction American politics will take as it enters the twenty-first century but also the direction American politics has already taken.

The series addresses the role of interest groups and social and political movements; openness in American politics; important developments in institutions such as the executive, legislative, and judicial branches at all levels of government as well as the bureaucracies thus created; the changing behavior of politicians and political parties; the role of public opinion; and the functioning of mass media. Because problems drive politics, the series also examines important policy issues in both domestic and foreign affairs.

The series welcomes all theoretical perspectives, methodologies, and types of evidence that answer important questions about trends in American politics.

AFRICAN AMERICAN LEGISLATORS IN THE AMERICAN STATES

Kerry L. Haynie

COLUMBIA UNIVERSITY PRESS
NEW YORK

Columbia University Press
Publishers Since 1893
New York   Chichester, West Sussex

Library of Congress Cataloging-in-Publication Data

Haynie, Kerry Lee.
    African American legislators in the American states / Kerry L.
Haynie.
        p. cm. — (Power, conflict, and democracy)
    Includes bibliographical references and index.
    ISBN 0–231–10644–0 (cloth : alk. paper) — ISBN 0–231–10645–9
(pbk. : alk. paper)
        1. African American state legislators.   2. Legislators—United
States—States.   3. Political planning—United States—States.   I. Title
II. Series.
    JK2488 .H39 2001
    328. 73′092′396073—dc21

                                                    00–069379

Casebound editions of Columbia University Press books are printed on permanent
and durable acid-free paper.
Printed in the United States of America
c 10 9 8 7 6 5 4 3 2 1
p 10 9 8 7 6 5 4 3 2 1

To my parents Joe and Nettie,
and to my siblings Melvin, Scott, Tony, and Lisa

CONTENTS

ACKNOWLEDGMENTS

I am indebted to a number of friends and colleagues who helped make this book possible. George Rabinowitz deserves special recognition for the direction, advice, and encouragement that he provided from the beginning to the end of this project. Thad Beyle, William Keech, Stuart Elaine MacDonald, and Michael Munger gave me valuable comments and suggestions at the very early stages of my research. I thank Kathleen Bratton for her advice, support, and friendship. Kathleen and I collaborated in creating a state legislative database from which much of the data used in this book is taken. I benefited enormously from numerous conversations and debates with my friend Carol M. Swain. Ross Baker, Rick Lau, Jack Nagel, Leonard Ray, and Mina Silberberg commented on various portions of the manuscript and provided me with sound scholarly advice. I am grateful to Thomas Callaghy for recommending the manuscript to Columbia University Press.

I thank Mina, Katie G. Cannon, Dwayne Lee Pinkney, and Ufo Uzodike for listening to my frustrations and offering me their friendship, encouragement, and support over the years. They truly helped me finish this project. Debts of gratitude are also due to my dear friends Reid and Vickie Hilton for opening their home, lake, and blueberry patch to me. Their generosity allowed me to "escape" and to maintain a "real world" perspective.

I received generous financial support for this project from the Graduate

School and the Department of Political Science at the University of North Carolina at Chapel Hill, as well as from the Political Science Department at the University of Pennsylvania. More recently, I have benefited from a very supportive work environment at Rutgers University.

I thank John Michel and Robert Y. Shapiro, my editors at Columbia University Press, for their patience and guidance. John provided the ideal amount of hand-holding and tactful prodding. I also thank Roy Thomas for making sure that what I have written stands a chance of making sense to those who dare to read it. However, I alone take full responsibility for the book's content.

AFRICAN AMERICAN LEGISLATORS
IN THE AMERICAN STATES

CHAPTER 1

INTRODUCTION

RACE REPRESENTATIVES OR "RESPONSIBLE LEGISLATORS"?

Has the growing presence of African American representatives in state legislatures resulted in greater African American influence in state policy-making? That is, do African American representatives have a noticeable and distinctive effect on legislative institutions and the policies they produce? Do they articulate and advocate a race-based legislative agenda? Have African American legislators become more integrated or incorporated into the legislative process over time? How are black legislators viewed or perceived by their peers?

These are the primary questions addressed in this book. The answers to them are relevant and of some importance to both African American and American politics for a number of reasons. First, given this country's history of de jure and de facto racial segregation, discrimination, and disenfranchisement, especially at the state level, it is significant and relevant to democratic theory and our system of representative governance whether or not American political institutions are now open to influence from a class of persons that was once widely regarded and treated as beings "of an inferior order; and altogether unfit to associate with the white race either in social or political relations."[1]

Second, after passage of the 1965 Voting Rights Act, black politics was transformed from pressure or "protest" politics to the politics of electoral participation. This new politics has served as an impetus for African Americans to compete for and win public office. However, the *new black politics* has not simply been a struggle to be included. For many, inclusion was intended to be a means toward several substantive ends rather than merely a symbolic end unto itself. For example, it was widely expected that black inclusion would in some way be a vehicle for altering American political institutions and achieving significant changes in the political and socioeconomic conditions of black people.[2] In exploring answers to the above questions, we can, with more than thirty years of hindsight, provide at least a partial evaluation of whether the consequences of the "new black politics" have been more symbolic than substantive.

Finally, the questions raised here are important because, since the early 1970s, states have grown in importance as both actors and arenas for public policy-making. Beginning with the Nixon administration and continuing through the present, devolution and new federalism initiatives have resulted in the public's becoming more reliant on states for programs and services that have in the past been provided primarily by the national government (e.g., Medicaid, student aid grants, school lunch programs, community development grants, Aid to Families with Dependent Children, and environmental protection).[3] Many of these programs are seen as essential for improving the socioeconomic status of African Americans as a group. Consequently, state-level institutions have taken on a renewed importance for African Americans attempting to get their policy interests and needs met. As we begin the twenty-first century, black state legislators are perhaps becoming just as important in securing and protecting black interests as are those African Americans who serve in the United States Congress.

Since 1970, the number of African Americans elected to state legislatures has grown by more than 237 percent. Between 1970 and 1998, the number of African American state legislators nationwide increased from 168 to 567. Today, more than 7 percent of state legislative seats nationwide are held by African Americans—up from 2 percent in 1970 (Joint Center for Political and Economic Studies 1998). This growth notwithstanding, the scholarly literature on African American state legislators remains relatively small in quantity, especially when compared to the studies of African Americans in Congress. The extant research on this topic can be divided into two broad categories: studies that provide mostly biographical data and information on the conditions under which blacks were elected to office (e.g., Bullock 1975; Cavanagh and Stockton 1983; Cole 1976; Conyers and Wallace 1976; Grofman and Handley 1985), and studies that provide analytical insights into the representation styles and policy interests of black legislators (e.g., Bratton and Haynie 1992, 1999a; Button and Hedge 1993; Hamm, Harmel, and Thompson 1983; Hedge, Button, and Scher 1992; Herring 1990; McGriggs 1977; Miller 1990; Nelson 1991; Perry 1976). This book is meant to build upon and expand the latter body of research. It is one of the first book-length studies to examine analytically the behavior of African American state legislators by simultaneously considering multiple legislative sessions in more than one state. With this study, I do not profess to offer a general theory of African American legislative behavior. Instead, similar to the main objective of John Wahlke et al.'s classic 1962 book, *The Legislative System: Exploration in Legislative Behavior,* I examine several issues relative to the presence and behavior of African Americans in legislative institutions with the hope of providing an analytical framework from which such theories might later be developed (see Wahlke 1962:3–4).

In describing the parameters of their project, Wahlke and his colleagues wrote:

> The aim of research was not to construct descriptive accounts of the institutions and processes of legislation in the four states studied, or of the political forces and factors which operate from day to day through their legislatures. Nor was it to discover precisely what happened in these four states in a particular session or to acquire understanding of the unique historical events of those particular situations. *The objective, rather, was to gain knowledge about generic problems of legislative institutions and processes in American state government.* (Wahlke et al. 1962:4; emphasis added)

This book is written from a similar perspective. My principal aim is to provide general knowledge about the nature and consequences of African American representation in state legislatures. In so doing, the study sheds some light on the question of how open, receptive, and responsive an important political institution has been to the nation's largest, most politically cohesive, and (in terms of political and social development) most historically significant racial minority group.

The growth in African American representation in state legislatures originated, to a large degree, with the political mobilization efforts associated with the civil rights movement of the 1960s. One product of these mobilization efforts was passage of the Voting Rights Act of 1965. The Voting Rights Act is arguably one on the most significant pieces of legislation passed by Congress in the twentieth century. Not only did it lead to tremendous increases in the number of African American elected officials at all levels of government, it also contributed directly to the growth in African American influence in the overall electoral process.

In addition to these rising numbers, many scholars and political observers have argued that in order to maximize their effectiveness and influence, African American legislators must also practice a politics intended to be system-changing. That is, black representatives should advocate and seek support for programs that are directly targeted, at least in part, toward African Americans, and that are likely to result in "radical" changes in social and economic policies (e.g., Barker and Jones 1994; Guinier 1992; Pinderhughes 1987; Smith 1990, 1996; Walton and McLemore 1970). In other words, African American legislators are expected to be what St. Clair Drake and Horace Cayton (1945) called *race men* and *race women*. The concept of the race man/woman originated in the slavery era. The term itself, however, comes from Drake and Cayton's now famous ethnographic study of Chicago's African American community.[4] Race men/women were black leaders who emerged from and lived in a segregated society and whose primary loyalty and responsibility was to African Americans. Sociologist Elijah Anderson has written (1997) that "the birth of the race man came at a time when there was a caste-like system in the culture as a whole and a particular rigid wall of segregation between blacks and whites in terms of styles of life, behavior, culture, residence, and power. The race man flourished in that caste-like system" (117). Race men and women often behaved as though they carried the burdens and ordeals of the entire race on their shoulders, and in public they almost always chose to put matters of race above all other issues. Race representatives were interested in and intent upon advancing the entire African American community.

Although they no longer emerge from environments that are completely racially isolated and segregated, contemporary African American representatives are, nevertheless, usually elected from districts in which the majority of the voters and constituents are African American or members of various racial and ethnic groups. Coming from such jurisdictions, they are expected to formulate and enact public policies that serve the interests of black people. However, one of the many ironies of African American politics is that in seeking to formulate and enact policies that address the particular needs and interests of the black community, African American legislators must operate in a political system and within political institutions that are biased against drastic or revolutionary change, and where the advocacy of black interests may be incongruent with both policy successes and professional advancement (Barker and

Jones 1994; Bennett 1963; Dymally 1971; Friedman 1993). In legislatures, for example, appropriations and expenditure patterns are often fixed for the near to intermediate term, and incrementalism tends to be the norm for budgetary and other important changes. Historian Lerone Bennett (1963) has argued that these fundamental characteristics of the American political system—the norm of incrementalism and the bias against rapid change—make the tasks of African American politicians an impossibility:

> Black politics has been the art of the impossible, because black politics has been the art of trying to make fundamental change in a political system by using the structures and instruments that were designed to perpetuate that system. It has been the art of the impossible because it has been the art of trying to make a social revolution with moderate tools that were invented to prevent social revolution.[5]   (Bennett 1963:5)

In other words, the American political system itself presents African American political representatives with a dilemma. The political system and its institutions are designed and structured in ways that repel the very kinds of fundamental social and economic changes that African American representatives often must advocate.

In a now classic 1961 article, "Committee Assignments in the House of Representatives," Nicholas Masters described the prototype legislator who was most likely to succeed and advance in this type of system. He referred to this legislator as the "responsible legislator":

> A responsible legislator is one whose ability, attitudes, and relationships with his [or her] colleagues serve to enhance the prestige and importance of the House of Representatives. He [or she] has a basic fundamental respect for the legislative process and understands and appreciates its formal and informal rules. . . . He understands the pressures on the members with whom he cannot always agree and avoids pushing an issue to the point where his opponents may suffer personal embarrassment. *On specific issues, no matter how firm his convictions and no matter how great the pressures upon him, he demonstrates a willingness to compromise.* He is moderate, not so much in the sense of his voting record and his personal ideology, but rather in the sense of a moderate approach. . . . [A] responsible legislator is apparently one who does not believe that the [legislature] is the proper place to initiate drastic and rapid changes in the direction of public policy. On the contrary, he is more inclined to be a gradualist, and to see public policy as sort of a "synthesis of opposing viewpoints."   (Masters 1961:352; emphasis added)

Thus adherence to and respect for status quo norms and incremental change are qualities valued by legislative institutions. Legislators fitting this description are rewarded with prestigious committee assignments, the respect of other legislators, and perhaps ultimately, more influence and effectiveness in the legislative process (Asher 1975; Davidson and Oleszek 1989; Friedman 1993; Huitt 1961; Keefe and Ogul 1993; Matthews 1960; Rosenthal 1981, 1990).

Given the enormity and persistent nature of the economic and social problems facing large segments of the African American community, attempting to follow or adopt the characteristics, norms, and predominant traits of legislative institutions and the "responsible legislator" imposes significant constraints on African American representatives who are expected or may feel pressure to pursue black interests. As Sally Friedman (1993) has put it, "Because of the demands from atypical constituents, the potential for different personal priorities, and backgrounds in minority issues or alternative political situations, these legislators may face more conflicts. They may find it more difficult to meet . . . the requirements of a 'majority' institution. To the extent that they do, they may be perceived as failing to represent their own constituents or as selling out to moderates."[6] That is, the role of race representative may be incompatible with the demands, expectations, and pressures placed upon African American representatives by fellow legislators, political parties, and the legislature as an institution (Button 1989; Button and Scher 1984; Karnig and Welch 1980).[7] Consequently, the legislative life of black legislators, perhaps more so than with other representatives, involves a perpetual concern with achieving some kind of workable balance between representing racial group interests and pushing for fundamental institutional reform on the one hand, and advancing a more mainstream agenda and seeking greater incorporation or integration into the legislative process on the other. Thus in order to be effective in performing their day-to-day legislative duties, African American representatives must have in their repertoire the skills and ability to manage the conflicts and dilemmas that result from these seemingly incompatible representational roles.

MANAGING DUALITY: TOWARD AN
ANALYTICAL FRAMEWORK

In his classic 1903 book, *The Souls of Black Folk*, W. E. B. Du Bois provided an eloquent and profound exposition of what can be called a *duality dilemma* that has long characterized the day-to-day life of many African Americans.

The Negro is sort of a seventh son, born with a veil, and gifted with a second-sight in this American world. . . . *One ever feels his two-ness—an American, a Negro; two souls, two thoughts, two unreconciled strivings; two warring ideals in one dark body,* whose dogged strength alone keeps it from being torn asunder.

(Du Bois 1961:3; emphasis added)

The duality dilemma is rooted in the concurrent pressures and expectations associated with living, working, and participating in the dominant white society while attempting to maintain an identity and connection with the African American community.[8] Sociologist Elijah Anderson (1997) describes the dilemma as a "precarious balance" between being (or being viewed as) a "race man or a sellout" (116). He suggests that the burdens may be greatest on the African American professional class. As he puts it, "So many of these blacks face the dual pressures and expectations of being 'professionals' in a white world and of dealing with what it means to be African American in the 1990s" (115).

Some of the issues arising from the O. J. Simpson murder trial, and in particular, some of the experiences of former Los Angeles assistant district attorney Christopher Darden, an African American who was one of the principal prosecutors in the case, provide a good illustration of, and exemplify the pervasiveness of, this dilemma.

Somehow the Simpson trial became so much more than a simple legal determination of whether a rich celebrity, former athlete, and known wife beater had snapped and killed his former spouse and her friend. It became, among other things, a debate about different views of blackness, about whether blacks can afford the luxury of placing much faith in a "white" system of justice.

(Cose 1997:76–77)

Addressing the experiences of prosecutor Christopher Darden, Anderson writes:

Darden's dilemma, therefore, is one he shares with many African Americans. He was trying to serve two basically contradictory gods, that of black racial particularism and that of meritocracy and universalism. His attempt to serve either one at any given time could easily be interpreted as a betrayal by followers of the other. To be seen as fair in terms of the merits of the case, he had to bend over backwards to disassociate himself from racial particularism, which, in a universalistic courtroom, could only be construed as bias.

But in doing so, he risked his status as an authentic black man—and in the race man ideology, to be an authentic black man is to put the black race first.

(Anderson 1997:128)

This brief exposition of Du Bois's duality dilemma provides the foundation and context for this book, as well as a starting point for building a framework that can be used to examine, and perhaps better understand, the behavior of contemporary African American legislators, and possibly the behavior of other black elected officials as well. One of the underlying arguments of this book is that like African American professionals, African Americans in politics also face a duality dilemma. Post-civil rights movement African American legislators are conceivably the most prominent contemporary political example and manifestation of this duality phenomenon. African American representatives face the paradoxical expectation of being both protagonists and antagonists of the political system. That is, they are expected to simultaneously be race representatives and responsible legislators. African American legislators must somehow manage the precarious and difficult tasks of becoming integrated into legislative institutions while at the same time trying to transform them.

Legislators themselves are cognizant of this dilemma. For example, a report describing and summarizing the proceedings of a 1990 symposium on "Women, Black, and Hispanic State Elected Leaders" indicates that one of the main topics of discussion that emerged during the symposium was, "how women and minority officials are to balance the expectation that they will carry the banner for women's and minority issues with their obligation to represent all people in their constituencies" (Carroll 1991:3). Comments from two symposium participants exemplify the duality dilemma. As one state legislator commented:

In working within the system, are we supposed to turn around and stop fighting the very thing we had fought to get here? I worry about the attitude that says that now that you're there you should just become like everyone else and try not to correct those things that you came here to correct.

(Carroll 1991:4)

Another representative argued:

I personally think we've got to be doing banking and we've got to be doing insurance and we've got to be having an impact across the board. If we don't do that, then we limit ourselves. If you want to move in the system, I think you have to broaden your agenda and let people know that you care about their issues.   (Carroll 1991:4)

The conference report goes on to say that, "African-Americans and Latinos seemed to feel more pressure than women to pursue a policy agenda focused on members of their group, perhaps because there is greater cohesiveness among these minority groups than among women" (4).

African American state legislators have three viable options or strategies for managing this dilemma. One is that they can persist as race representatives, making matters on race their primary concern. However, by maintaining the posture of the race representative, African American state legislators run the risk of becoming something akin to what Huitt (1961) called legislative "outsiders." Outsiders are those legislators who sometimes may stand in opposition to their party, and who do not necessarily conform to the norms and traditions of the institution. For example, unlike with the responsible legislator role, whenever they deem it necessary, representatives who adopt or are forced into the role of outsider are willing to propose legislation that seeks drastic and rapid changes in the direction of existing public policy (Huitt 1961:571). A potential negative consequence associated with the outsider role is that legislators who are cast in it may become less effective and less influential in the policy process. They may be less able to forge winning or meaningful coalitions in support of their interests, and they may be less likely to garner the respect of their colleagues (Matthews 1960; White 1956; Wilson 1960).

A second option available to black legislators for managing the duality dilemma is to "deracialize" their legislative agendas in order to appeal to a more diverse audience, thereby making it easier for them to become integrated and incorporated into the legislative process.[9] Lucius Barker and Mack Jones (1994) define *deracialization* as "the practice of blacks articulating political demands in terms that are not racially specific so that they appeal to a broader group and presumably do not alienate those who are predisposed to oppose black efforts" (321). Similarly, McCormick (1989) writes, "The essence of this political strategy [deracialization] is that its proponents would seek to de-emphasize those issues that may be viewed in explicitly racial terms . . . while emphasizing those issues that appear to transcend the racial question" (quoted in McCormick and Jones 1993:72). Because it is usually connected to attempts at coalition-building, this strategy is often advocated as a useful means of integrating African Americans into political institutions and advancing the cause of black interests

(Hamilton 1977; Skocpol 1991; Swain 1993; Wilson 1987, 1990).[10] For example, in his provocative and highly acclaimed book, *The Truly Disadvantaged,* William Julius Wilson (1987) advocates comprehensive "universal" programs, as opposed to "race-specific or group-specific strategies," as prudent means by which to meaningfully address the problems of the so-called African American urban underclass.[11] Wilson (1990) offered similar advice to the Democratic Party as a strategy for putting together winning presidential election coalitions.

> In the 1990s the party needs to promote new policies to fight inequality that differ from court-ordered busing, affirmative action programs, and anti-discrimination lawsuits of the recent past. By stressing coalition politics and *race neutral* programs such as full employment strategies, job skills training, comprehensive health care, reforms in the public schools, child care legislation, and prevention of crime and drug abuse, the Democrats can significantly strengthen their position.   (Wilson 1990:74; emphasis added)

While on the one hand, deracialization may be a useful strategy for integrating African Americans into political institutions, increasing the level of African American incorporation in legislatures, and achieving enactment of broadbased programs that provide residual benefits to blacks, on the other it may prove to be counterproductive when it comes to efforts to pass the requisite legislation and enact the necessary public policies that might stimulate significant and immediate changes in the socioeconomic conditions of African American citizens. In other words, race-related or racially laden problems may require race-conscious or race-specific solutions. Moreover, Barker and Jones (1994) provide a persuasive argument that deracialization may contribute to the "routinization" of black politics in which African American political participation becomes more "system supporting" rather than "system challenging" (322).

The third strategy available to African American legislators is a sort of middle-ground approach with which legislators recognize the significance of racial differences and acknowledge that race matters, but at the same time they also seek to address issues of broader concern. This middle-ground strategy blends elements of both the race representative and deracialization approaches. It involves efforts by legislators to balance the pressures and expectation that they simultaneously be race representatives and "responsible legislators." This strategy is consistent with what David Canon (1999) calls the "balancing perspective" (48). With the balancing perspective, African American legislators pursue

TABLE 1.1

AFRICAN AMERICANS IN THE LEGISLATURES

State/Year	No. of African Americans in Legislature	% African Americans in Legislature	% African Americans in State	Majority Party in Legislature*
Arkansas				
1969	0	0.0	18.3	**D**
1979	3	3.0	16.3	**D**
1989	5	5.0	16.9	**D**
Illinois				
1969	14	7.9	12.8	R
1979	14	7.9	14.7	R
1989	14	11.7	14.8	**D**
Maryland				
1969	8	5.6	17.8	**D**
1979	14	9.9	22.7	**D**
1989	22	15.6	25.7	**D**
New Jersey				
1969	5	6.3	10.8	R
1979	4	3.7	12.5	**D**
1989	6	7.1	14.3	R
North Carolina				
1969	1	0.8	22.0	**D**
1979	2	1.7	22.4	**D**
1989	13	10.8	22.3	**D**

*Bold indicates African Americans in the majority party.

a black interest agenda without resorting to "the divisive language of sepa-ratism." The balancing approach allows the representative to recognize and re-spond to the fact that African Americans and other constituents do not have all the same interests (Canon 1999:47–49). Canon cites the example of affirmative action, which sometimes requires legislators to take a position that will alienate some segment of·their constituency. In such a case, the balancing representa-tive attempts to offset such a controversial stand by also working on issues that have no race-specific content (ibid., 50).

Much of the data used in the analyses that follow comes from a data set con-structed by Kathleen A. Bratton and myself (Bratton and Haynie 1999). Specif-ically, the data come from the 1969, 1979, and 1989 legislative sessions of the lower house of five state legislatures: Arkansas, Illinois, Maryland, New Jersey, and North Carolina.[12] The time period covered is significant because it encompasses the critical period of growth in African American representation. Furthermore, as can be seen in table 1.1, the selected states and years provide regional diversity, variance in the ratio of percent black in the population to the percent black in the legislature, and variance in party control of the legislature.[13] It is important to account for regional diversity because, similar to an argument made by Sue Thomas (1991) regarding the study of women legislators, any policy or behavioral differences found to exist between African American and other legislators could be attributed to the fact that certain political cultures are more or less supportive of black interests or race-related matters regardless of the race of the legislator or the percentage of African Americans in the legislature. This is not to suggest, however, that these five legislatures are a representative sample of any particular region or of the entire universe of state legislatures. Nevertheless, exploring the behavior and experiences of African Americans legislators in these states will perhaps contribute to a foundation on which important theoretical generalizations can be built.

In the subsequent chapters of this book, I provide empirical analyses of how African Americans in state legislatures have behaved in their efforts to substantively represent black interests. In addition, I examine whether or not, and to what extent, these legislators have become incorporated into the legislative institution. In so doing, I pay particular attention to how they manage the duality dilemmas they face while attempting to make a distinctive impact on public policy. That is, I seek to determine whether the African American lawmakers have behaved more like race representatives or responsible legislators or whether they have attempted to strike a balance between these two perspectives. Also, in a case study of one of the legislatures, I explore the issue of how African American legislators are viewed or perceived by their peers.

Specifically, chapter 2 looks at the introduction of proposed legislation by, or the agenda-setting behavior of, black legislators. The objectives of this chapter are to determine whether African American state lawmakers have a noticeable and distinctive effect on legislative agendas, to determine if there is a significant correlation between descriptive and substantive representation, and to examine whether, in their agenda-setting behavior, black legislators behave in a manner that is characteristic of the race men and women of Drake and Cayton's *Black Metropolis* (1945).

In chapter 3 the focus remains on discerning the nature of the representation that African American legislators provide their African American constituents, but here the empirical analyses concern their standing committee assignment patterns. Given the central role that committees play in legislatures, an examination of committee assignments provides us with another important venue from which to evaluate the behavior of African American legislators. The simple presence of African Americans in legislatures or even their articulation of a race-based agenda may not be sufficient if they are to have significant influence in public policy-making. Several studies have shown that African American officeholders must achieve *political incorporation* as a precondition to having a meaningful effect on government policies and programs. Political incorporation refers to the extent to which a group is strategically positioned to exercise significant influence over the policy-making process. Chapter 4 investigates whether or not African American representatives have achieved meaningful levels of political incorporation in the five legislatures. I construct an African American "political incorporation index" that is suited especially for legislatures. The scale is weighted in favor of leadership positions, seniority, and strategic institutional positioning. African American political incorporation scores were computed for all three legislative sessions in each of the five states. Whether or not higher levels of incorporation are beneficial to black legislators and black interests is one of the primary questions addressed in this chapter.

A case study that explores how African American legislators are perceived and evaluated by their peers is the subject of chapter 5. I use evaluations of legislative effectiveness as measures of perception. This analysis is limited to only the North Carolina General Assembly because appropriate and comparable data do not exist for the other legislatures. A more detailed description and explanation of this data can be found in chapter 5.

Finally, in chapter 6, I summarize the overall findings, discuss their significance for theory and practice, and speculate about future trends. I also present relevant and related questions that remain unanswered, yet are worthy of exploration in future studies.

CHAPTER 2

AGENDA-SETTING AND THE REPRESENTATION OF BLACK INTERESTS

One of the most important consequences of the 1960s civil rights movement has been the increased presence of African Americans in elected positions at all levels of government. Many of those involved or associated with the civil rights movement recognized that in order to secure meaningful political rights, equal treatment before the law, and economic opportunity, and in order to maximize African Americans' potential to affect public policy, it was necessary for African Americans to compete for and win public office. As political scientists James Button and Richard Scher put it, "If they [African Americans] were to achieve true political capabilities, they could not remain on the outside looking in, but had to insure that blacks became a part of political decision-making processes at local, state, and national levels" (1984:184). Similarly, Charles Bullock, a long-time student of black politics, has argued:

> While political participation may elicit concessions from white officeholders, they may respond racially when white and black interests conflict. . . . Moreover, even well-meaning white politicians may be unable to comprehend some black needs and therefore fail to introduce them into the policy-making arena. Consequently, adequate representation of black demands . . . requires that there be black officeholders to translate these demands into policy. (Bullock 1975:727)

Thus, historically, African American legislators have been expected to change not only how legislatures look but also what they produce. The emergence and growth of African American representation in legislatures has raised considerable expectations that African American lawmakers would address issues of particular importance to African American citizens, whose interests may not have been adequately addressed in these institutions before there was a significant black presence. In other words, there has been the expectation and hope that African Americans serving in policy-making institutions would provide substantive representation for African American citizens.

To provide substantive representation means to act "in the interest of the represented in a manner that is responsive to them" (Pitkin 1967:209). Substantive representation is the degree of congruence between the actions and behavior of a representative and the policy preferences of her or his constituents. It concerns what the representative does rather than what or who he or she is. Substantive representation is often contrasted with descriptive representation, which simply focuses on the degree to which a representative reflects or mirrors the distinctive social characteristics of the constituents that he or she represents—characteristics like race, ethnicity, gender, social class, or religion. In the case of descriptive representation, the emphasis is on who or what the representative is, rather than on what he or she may actually do.[1]

Academics, journalists, African American constituents, and other legislators have all presumed that black legislators would provide African Americans with substantive representation by articulating and advocating something called "the black interest," and that these legislators would be agents of economic, social, and political advancement for *all* black citizens, regardless of where those citizens happened to reside (e.g., Barker and Jones 1994; Barnett 1975; Bratton and Haynie 1999a; Bullock 1975; Button 1989; Button and Scher 1984; Campbell and Feagin 1975; Conyers and Wallace 1976; McCormick and Jones 1993; McGriggs 1977). State Representative Dan Blue, an African American from North Carolina, put it this way: "As more minorities once again sit in the room where government decisions are made, their participation will give blacks a better chance at fair treatment in state policies. Their presence can help shape the state's role in economic development and its response to social ills such as poverty, failing education programs, crime, and the lack of affordable health care."[2] In other words, the prevailing presumption has been that African American elected officials would and perhaps should behave like the "race representatives" historically found in African American communities (e.g., Bratton and Haynie 1999a; Guinier 1991, 1992; Smith 1996; Walters 1992). Recall from chapter 1 that race representatives are those leaders and officials whose primary goal is to advance the interests of the black community. When operating outside of their community, and especially when they serve in political or policy-making institutions, race representatives attempt to insure that a "black perspective" is articulated and understood (Drake and Cayton 1945).

Do African American state legislators meet these expectations? Can they be classified as race representatives? Have they articulated and advocated a race-based or race-related set of legislative issues? Is there in fact a connection between descriptive and substantive representation? This chapter addresses these questions by examining the bills that African American state legislators introduce. The aim of this examination is threefold: first, to determine whether African American state lawmakers have a noticeable and distinctive effect on legislative agendas; second, to determine if there is a significant correlation between descriptive and substantive representation; and third, to examine whether, in their agenda-setting behavior, the black legislators behave as prototype race representatives.

THEORETICAL JUSTIFICATIONS

The expectations that African American representatives would have a distinctive impact on legislative agendas and behave as race men and race women is not merely a reflection of symbolic politics. These expectations are also rooted in theories of political participation, group identity politics, and political representation. For example, it has long been a maxim in American politics that political participation results in rewards and benefits from the system. Since the passage of the 1965 Voting Rights Act, there have been significant increases in African American participation in politics. Moreover, the gap between African American and white voter registration and turnout rates is smaller today than it was during the period immediately preceding the Voting Rights Act (e.g., Davidson 1992; Davidson and Grofman 1994; Grofman and Davidson 1992; Gurin, Hatchett, and Jackson 1989; Lawson 1985; Reeves 1997). Thus it is reasonable to expect that black Americans would reap some tangible and substantive benefits from this increased involvement in the governmental process. Indeed, several studies have demonstrated that increased African American political participation *is* responsible for gains in both descriptive and substantive representation of African Americans in government and public policy (Bullock 1975, 1981; Combs, Hibbing, and Welch 1984; Grofman and Handley 1989; Herring 1990; Keech 1968; McClain 1990; Whitby 1985; 1987; Whitby and Gilliam 1991). Studies by Kenny Whitby and Franklin Gilliam Jr. (1991) and Mary Herring (1990), for example, found greater African American political mobilization to be related to increased legislative support of black interests.

Regarding representation theory, from the vast body of research on the representative-constituency relationship, we know that in general there is a convergence between the interests of constituents and the behavior of representatives. This is particularly true with the most salient issues (Erickson 1978; Fenno 1978; Jewell 1983; Miller and Stokes 1963; Stone 1979).[3] For example, regarding two issues that have long resonated widely among the general public—civil rights and welfare issues—Stone (1979) found high correlations between constituency opinion and the roll-call behavior of members of Congress. These findings and the larger representative-constituency literature suggest a constituency representation model in which race or other descriptive characteristics of a representative has little independent impact on legislative behavior (e.g., see Bratton and Haynie 1999a:658–59). Yet, given that the overwhelming majority of African American legislators represent majority black districts, this model, nevertheless, yields the logical and reasonable expectation that they will provide their African American constituents with race-based substantive representation.[4]

In his 1994 book, *Behind the Mule: Race and Class in African-American Politics,* Michael Dawson develops what he calls a "black utility heuristic"—a sociopsychological theoretical framework for analyzing black politics that relates the political beliefs and behavior of individual African Americans to their perception of racial group interests. Dawson demonstrates that there are high levels of cohesion and consistency among African Americans on public opinion and policy preferences, and he argues that the link between an individual black person's perception of his or her own interests and the same individual's sense of the racial group is the key to this seemingly politically solidary black community.[5]

Whitby (1997) suggests that a logical conclusion of Dawson's *black utility heuristic* is the expectation that an overwhelming majority of African American elected officials will behave in a manner that is similar to the race representatives described earlier in this book. Whitby argues that, based on Dawson's model, most African American officeholders

> will have a strong sense of racial identity, which will lead them to support policies of interests to black constituents. In some sense a spontaneous form

of representation will emerge because of the development of a unique racial consciousness and belief system that makes black representatives predisposed to vote the way most blacks in the district would want the legislator to vote anyway. In essence their support for black policy preferences should be unparalleled . . . because what's in the best interest of the black masses is also in the best interest of black policymakers.   (Whitby 1997:83)

As the above brief sketch suggests, the combined existing literature exploring black political participation, group identity, and legislative representation provides a strong theoretical basis for the expectation that African American legislators will behave as race men and women by advancing a race-based legislative agenda and providing substantive representation for black interests. Before turning to an empirical examination of this conjecture, however, a discussion of "black interests" is in order.

What Are Black Interests?

Because *interest,* in social science usage, is a contested concept (that is, it has no single widely agreed upon meaning), then determining or designating a group's interests is usually a complex and complicated undertaking.[6] Nevertheless, social scientists routinely seek to identify, measure, and evaluate such interests. Most estimates of a group's interests involve both objective and subjective elements. Measurable socioeconomic phenomena like unemployment, poverty rates, income, and educational levels are often used as "objective" indicators of a group's interests (Sargent 1991; Swain 1993; Whitby 1987). Subjective interests are less observable and more difficult to evaluate because they involve the feelings, emotions, and temperaments of the individuals or group in question. Surveys and public opinion polls, however, provide useful tools for identifying the subjective interests of groups.

Determining *black interests* may be a much simpler task than defining the interests of other groups. Notwithstanding the fact that blacks are not monolithic in their attitudes, beliefs, and values, a shared culture, the legacy of slavery, and the historical significance of race in the United States provide African Americans with many common political interests and goals. In fact, on questions of public policy, ideology, and candidate choice, African Americans have been the most cohesive and consistent political subgroup in U.S. politics (Bullock 1984; Dawson 1994; Gurin, Hatchett, and Jackson 1989; Lewis and Schneider 1983; Tate 1993). Using objective and subjective components, I will offer a definition of "black interests" as they have commonly been perceived by both researchers and African American citizens.

OBJECTIVE INDICATORS OF BLACK INTERESTS

Annual reports of the socioeconomic conditions of African Americans repeatedly show that black Americans have relatively low and unequal socioeconomic status when compared to whites (Dewart 1988, 1989, 1990, 1991; Tidwell 1992). These reports indicate that over the last two decades of the twentieth century, there have been few consistent improvements in the relative economic position of the African American population as a whole. This is not to say that the economic situation for all African Americans has remained the same. In fact, many studies reveal a growing black middle class and demonstrate that some individual African Americans fare better than others (Dawson 1994; Gurin, Hatchett, and Jackson 1989; U.S. Department of Commerce 1992). It remains the case, however, that African Americans as a group are less well-off than the white majority.

> In comparison to Americans of European descent, African Americans experience substantially lower economic status throughout the income distribution [and] . . . relatively well-off blacks are much less well-off than well-off whites, and relatively poor blacks are much poorer than poor whites.
>
> (Swinter 1992:61).

Table 2.1 contains unemployment statistics for selected years between 1980 and 1990. While on a downward trend, black unemployment remained high throughout the entire period. Moreover, in each of the years, the African American unemployment rate is more than twice that of whites.

Income levels are directly related to unemployment rates. Table 2.2 contains

TABLE 2.1
BLACK AND NONBLACK UNEMPLOYMENT RATES, 1980–1990

	1980	1984	1986	1988	1990
Black	14.3%	15.9	14.5	11.7	11.3
White	6.3%	6.5	6.0	4.7	4.7

Source: U.S. Department of Commerce 1991: table 635.

TABLE 2.2

MEDIAN HOUSEHOLD INCOME, 1970–1990 (IN 1990 DOLLARS)

Year	Black	White	B/W Ratio
1970	$18,652	$30,644	60.8
1975	17,997	29,978	60.0
1977	18,164	30,781	59.0
1979	18,242	31,071	58.7
1981	16,261	28,977	56.1
1983	16,368	28,915	56.6
1985	18,000	30,255	59.4
1987	18,031	31,591	57.1
1989	19,060	32,049	59.5
1990	18,676	31,231	59.8

Source: U.S. Department of Commerce 1991: table 635. (B/W ratio [black to white ratio] calculations done by author.)

data on median household income. In 1990, African American households had a median income of $18,676. This was a $384 decrease from 1989 and only a $24 increase over the 1970 amount. On the other hand, white household median income increased $587 between 1970 and 1990. Overall, black family income has been flat since 1970 and was generally lower during the 1980s than it was in the 1970s.

As the B/W (black to white ratio) index in table 2.2 indicates, household income inequality increased during the twenty years covered. For example, in 1970, Africa American median household income was 60.9 percent of the median household income of white families; by 1990 it was 59.8 percent.

Income disadvantages and inequalities contribute to African Americans' experiencing significantly higher levels of poverty than whites. Every year between 1970 and 1990, nearly one-third of all African Americans were impoverished (table 2.3).[7] The statistics on black poverty are more dramatic when we look at poverty among children (table 2.4). In 1990, 44.2 percent of all African American children lived in poverty. Moreover, the poverty rate for African American children was at least three times the poverty rate for white children in all but two years (1983 and 1990) during the 1970–1990 period. In these two years, however, the poverty rate for black children was still more than twice the rate for white children.

Education is often touted as a means to avoid or escape poverty and as a pri-

TABLE 2.3

PERSONS BELOW THE POVERTY LEVEL, 1970–1990

Year	Black	White
1970	33.5%	9.9%
1975	31.3	9.7
1977	31.3	8.9
1979	31.0	9.0
1981	34.2	11.1
1983	35.7	12.1
1985	31.3	11.4
1987[a]	32.4	10.4
1989	30.7	10.0
1990	31.9	10.7

Source: U.S. Department of Commerce 1991: table 717.
[a]Beginning in 1987, percentages are based on revised processing procedures and the data are not directly comparable with prior years.

TABLE 2.4

CHILDREN BELOW THE POVERTY LEVEL, 1970–1990

Year	Black	White
1970	41.5%	10.5%
1975	41.4	12.5
1977	41.6	11.4
1979	40.8	11.4
1981	44.9	14.7
1983	46.2	17.0
1985	43.1	15.6
1987[a]	44.4	14.7
1989	43.2	14.1
1990	44.2	15.1

Source: U.S. Department of Commerce 1991: table 718.
[a]Beginning in 1987, percentages are based on revised processing procedures and the data are not directly comparable with prior years.

TABLE 2.5

PERCENT OF POPULATION, 25 YEARS OLD AND OLDER
(WITH LESS THAN 12 YEARS OF SCHOOL AND WITH 4 OR MORE
YEARS OF COLLEGE), 1970–1990

	<12 Years of School			4 or More Years of College		
Race	1970	1980	1990	1970	1980	1990
Black	68.6%	48.8	33.0	4.4	8.4	11.3
White	45.5%	31.2	20.9	11.3	17.1	22.0

Source: U.S. Department of Commerce 1991: table 222.

mary vehicle for African Americans to move into the middle and upper classes. While there were significant improvements during the two-and-a-half decades cited, educational achievement among African Americans continues to lag woefully behind that of whites. For example, the data in table 2.5 show that in 1990, one-third of all African Americans had completed fewer than twelve years of school and only 11.3 percent had completed four or more years of college. For whites the numbers were 20.1 and 22.2 percent, respectively.

SUBJECTIVE INDICATORS OF BLACK INTERESTS

Opinion polls and surveys provide some information about what policies and programs African Americans desire. Such data serve as indicators of the subjective interests of blacks. For example, the 1984–1988 National Black Election Panel Study found that 88 percent of African Americans agreed that the government should work to improve the position of blacks, and 82 percent favored increased government spending for job creation. This study also found that 79 percent of African Americans were in favor of more spending for Medicare and 50 percent favored increased support for food stamps (see Dawson 1994:190–91; Gurin, Hatchett, and Jackson:88). Similarly, when asked in a 1992 study, "Which one or two issues mattered most in deciding how you voted?" African Americans ranked the economy first, health care second, and education third (Keene et al. 1993:93).

It is important to note that African American public opinion on policy preferences is consistent across social classes. In one of the most thorough examinations of African American political attitudes and policy preferences, Gurin, Hatchett, and Jackson write that

the most important conclusion to be drawn from our analyses is that this
was a solidary electorate in two senses: blacks from all walks of life had similar political goals and policy preferences and also felt a sense of racial soli-
darity. There was certainly no evidence that middle-class blacks were dissoci-
ated from problems of the black community.[8]   (1989:117)

Similarly, Michael Dawson (1994) concludes that

within the realm of mainstream American partisan politics, African-American political behavior remains powerfully influenced by African Americans'
perceptions of group interests. What is perceived as good for the group still
plays a dominant role in shaping African-American partisanship, political
choice, and public opinion. *Perceptions of group interests are not associated
with economic status.* Within the confines of mainstream American politics,
*individual economic status plays a small role in shaping African-American po-
litical choice.*[9]   (1994:204–205; emphasis added)

With information like the above socioeconomic and public opinion data, it
is possible to define "black interests" in a way that takes into account both its
objective and subjective components. These data depict an economically and
socially disadvantaged African American community, and they provide some
insights into how blacks themselves view their situation. Thus it is reasonable
to posit that improving their economic and social conditions is in the interests
of African Americans. To this end, *black interests,* as used in this book, will
be defined as support for legislation and policies favoring social welfare, economic redistribution, and civil rights issues. Specifically, laws that prohibit discrimination in voting, housing, education, and unemployment, and laws that
support unemployment compensation, jobs programs, food stamps, and educational assistance are considered to be black interests.

INTRODUCTIONS OF BILLS AND LEGISLATIVE AGENDA-SETTING

Proposing new laws is one of the most basic functions that legislators perform.
Introducing legislation provides legislators with the opportunity to place policy initiatives on legislative agendas. Legislative agendas are the sets of issues
and policy initiatives debated by the legislature as a whole. They are the various
issues at the center of controversy at any given time (see, for example, Cobb

and Elder 1983; Kingdon 1984; Sinclair 1981; and Walker 1977). Making a contribution to and having an effect on the agenda-setting process is of considerable importance to legislators.

> The choice of issues for debate is of central importance in any political system. By deciding what they will decide about, legislators also establish the terms and the most prominent participants in the debate and, ultimately, the distribution of power and influence in the society.   (Walker 1977:423)

Similarly, E. E. Schattschneider (1960) argues that "*the definition of the alternatives is the supreme instrument of power*. . . . He [or she] who determines what politics is about runs the country, because the definition of alternatives is the choice of conflicts and the choice of conflicts allocates power" (68; italics in original). Thus through their bill introductions, African American legislators have the opportunity to make a noticeable and distinctive impact in state legislatures, and to exert substantial influence on state policy-making by placing black interest issues on legislative agendas.

R. Douglas Arnold (1990) has argued that analyzing legislators' bill introductions is often superior to a reliance on roll-call votes for attempting to establish a linkage between constituency interests or preferences and the legislative behavior of representatives. Like Schattschneider, he suggests that "the power of the electoral connection may actually be greater at earlier stages of decision making, when legislators are deciding which problems to pursue or which alternatives to consider, rather than at the final stages, when legislators are voting on particular amendments or on a bill's final passage" (269). To illustrate and support this assertion, Arnold chronicles parts of the legislative histories of the nuclear freeze resolutions that were considered in the U.S. House of representatives in 1982 and 1983, as well as the 1986 congressional debate over tax reform. He concludes: "Unfortunately for those who assess constituency influence by analyzing roll-call votes, virtually all of the relevant decisions were made early in the legislative process, behind closed doors, and without recorded votes" (271).[10]

Bill introductions from the 1969, 1979, and 1989 legislative sessions of the lower house of the Arkansas, Illinois, Maryland, New Jersey, and North Carolina legislatures provide the data for this analysis.[11] Again, bill introductions are important because, unlike roll-call votes, they detail what representatives actually add to the policy agenda. And getting items on legislative agendas for serious debate is a prerequisite for getting them enacted. Moreover, bill introductions can serve as a thermometer for gauging the intensity of commitments to particular interests (Di Lorenzo 1997).

The various state legislative journals were used so that all the bills introduced in these five states during the three legislative sessions could be coded and categorized based on their substantive content.[12] Many bills were placed into more than one category. For example, a bill to provide for the increased desegregation of a state university system was coded as both an education and civil rights issue. Any bill that, in the judgment of the author, hindered the social, political, or economic progress of African Americans was excluded from all categories. Although bills could have multiple sponsors, only primary sponsors are included as introducers.

Based on the definition of black interests given above, the primary focus is on bill introductions in five broad categories: education, health care, poverty/social welfare, civil rights, and children's issues. The education bills category includes all proposals that regulate, finance, or improve a state's system of public schools, and laws that pertain to the administering of colleges and universities. Legislation involving scholarships and student financial aid programs are also included in this category. Health care bills include a variety of bills relating to the physical and mental welfare of citizens, as well as public health issues like contagious disease control, occupational illnesses, and environment-related health hazards. In the social welfare category are proposals that are intended to alleviate poverty. This includes measures that provide monetary subsidies and programmatic services like jobs training, food stamps, low-income housing, and medical assistance to the poor or otherwise disadvantaged. Minimum-wage legislation is also included in the social welfare category. Civil rights legislation constitutes laws that expressly prohibit discrimination on account of race, gender, ethnicity, religion, age, disability, national origin, or sexual orientation. Finally, among children's issues are bills that provide child and youth services (e.g., recreation, jobs programs, etc.), and laws that seek to protect minors from various forms of abuse.

ADVOCACY OF BLACK INTERESTS

Who promotes black interests in state legislatures? Table 2.6 contains data comparing black interest bill introduction activity by African American and nonblack legislators. In each of the three legislative sessions, a majority (from 55 to 82 percent) of African American representatives introduced black interest

TABLE 2.6

COMPARISON OF BLACK INTEREST BILL INTRODUCTIONS BY RACE

	% of African Americans Who Introduce a Black Interest Bill	% of Whites Who Introduce a Black Interest Bill
1969	82	39
1979	55	7
1989	82	22
Total	74	23

Source: Bratton and Haynie 1999a.
Note: As used in this table, black interest bills include introductions in civil rights, education, health care, and poverty/social welfare issues as well as children's and women's issues. The percentages are based on data pooled from each of the five states.

legislation.[13] In only one year, however, did more than a quarter of nonblack legislators introduce at least one black interest bill. In each instance, at least twice as many African Americans than nonblack legislators introduced black interest legislation.

In table 2.7, I compare African American and other legislators in terms of the percentage of their total number of bill introductions that was devoted to black interest legislation. These data are reported by state and year. North Carolina's 1979 and 1989 legislative sessions are the only cases in which black interest bills are a majority of African Americans' total introductions. However, in all but one of the legislative sessions (New Jersey 1969), the proportion of bills that African American legislators dedicated to black interest issues was greater than that of nonblack representatives. The differences are statistically significant in thirteen of the fifteen legislative sessions.

The data in tables 2.6 and 2.7 clearly show that African American state legislators are the primary advocates for black interests. In each of the sampled states and years, a majority (55–82 percent) of African American representatives introduced at least one piece of black interest legislation. These data also show that African American legislators do not focus exclusively on racial issues. In fact, it was in only two out of the fourteen legislative sessions considered that a majority of the bills introduced by African Americans focused on such issues. Yet when a black interest bill is introduced, it is at least twice as likely to be introduced by an African American legislator than by a nonblack one. Also,

TABLE 2.7

BLACK INTEREST BILL INTRODUCTIONS AS A PERCENTAGE OF ALL
BILL INTRODUCTIONS

| State/Year | Proposed by | | Difference |
	Blacks	Nonblacks	
Arkansas			
1979	20.8	19.5	1.3
1989	39.4	23.5	15.9*
Illinois			
1969	27.5	9.1	18.4*
1979	30.8	17.4	13.4*
1989	39.6	9.8	29.8*
Maryland			
1969	46.6	18.5	28.1*
1979	28.6	25.3	3.3
1989	37.7	29.2	8.5*
New Jersey			
1969	14.8	16.1	−1.3
1979	31.6	18.1	13.5*
1989	37.9	23.9	14.0*
North Carolina			
1969	40.0	13.1	26.9*
1979	75.0	16.9	58.1*
1989	53.1	26.3	26.8*

*Black-white difference significant at the .01 level.

African American legislators tend to devote a greater proportion of their introductions to black interest issues than other representatives.

Is It Race That Explains the Difference?

The finding that African American legislators tend to disproportionately introduce black interest legislation gives rise to an interesting and important question: are these differences in agenda-setting behavior in any way attributable to
the legislators' race? That is, is there a significant correlation between the descriptive presence of African Americans in the legislature and the substantive
representation of black interests?

In an earlier study, Kathleen A. Bratton and I (Bratton and Haynie 1999a), examined the effects of gender and race on legislative agenda-setting. Using data from the same data set and some of the analyses from that earlier study, here I focus exclusively on the impact of race. Regression analysis is used to assess what effects, if any, race has on bill introductions. The unit of analysis is the individual legislator, and the dependent variable is the number of bills introduced in a particular category in a given year and state. Because the dependent variable is an event count, using negative binomial regression is in order (see King 1988, 1989).[14]

In addition to the race of the legislator, *gender, party affiliation,* and *seniority* are also included as explanatory variables. Democrats and women tend to have more liberal attitudes than Republicans and men toward social and economic policies and government spending in general, and therefore party affiliation and gender might influence the substantive content of a legislator's bill introductions (Jacobson 1992).[15] Because seniority is a likely contributor to expertise in certain policy areas, and because more senior legislators are more likely to have greater skill at navigating the legislative labyrinth (Hibbing 1991, 1993; Meyer 1980; Weissert 1989), I include seniority as a potential explanatory variable. Seniority is measured as the number of consecutive years in the legislature.

Because districts with high percentages of blacks may be more likely to elect a representative who will be supportive of black interests regardless of his or her race, I control for the racial composition of the district, measured as the *percentage of blacks in the district logged.* There is also a control for *whether or not the district is majority black.*[16]

Given the distinctive set of socioeconomic problems that disproportionately affect urban areas (e.g., high unemployment, concentrated pockets of poverty, higher rates of HIV/AIDS, etc.), legislators from urban districts might be inclined to introduce legislation related to these policy areas regardless of their race. Thus *urbanness* is included as an explanatory variable.[17] Recognizing that predominantly African American districts in urban areas might be different from mostly white urban districts and predominantly black districts in rural areas (Combs, Hibbing, and Welch 1984; Whitby 1985), I also control for the interaction between urbanness and the percentage of blacks in the district.

Standing committees are the principal organizational units in legislatures. Not only do they have disproportionate power over the policy areas in their respective jurisdictions, committees also have significant influence over the entire legislative process (e.g., Fenno 1973; Francis 1989; Grier and Munger 1991; Hedlund and Powers 1987; Keefe and Ogul 1993; Rhode and Shepsle 1973; Rosenthal 1974; Shepsle 1988; Smith and Deering 1984). Because of the central role that committees play, I include *membership on relevant committees* as an additional explanatory variable.

Results and Discussion

On the question of whether there is a connection between a descriptive presence of African Americans in legislatures and the substantive representation of black interests, the regression results in table 2.8 demonstrate that the answer is an unequivocal yes. These data show that the race of the representative has a powerful and statistically significant effect on the introduction of traditional civil rights legislation. That is, African Americans, all else being equal, were significantly more likely than nonblack legislators to introduce bills that prohibited racial discrimination in education, employment, and housing, and laws that expressly advanced the socioeconomic well-being of African Americans. Furthermore, *race* was a significant factor for the introduction of bills in two of the other four black interest categories—education and social welfare policy. In both cases, the regression coefficient for race was the largest in terms of magnitude of effect.

Gender, membership on relevant committees, and party affiliation are other personal characteristics that influenced whether a legislator introduced black interest bills. Having an assignment on a committee whose jurisdiction included black interest issues had a significant positive effect on a representative's propensity to introduce these bills. Women and Democrats were more likely than men and Republicans to propose such legislation. It is interesting and important to note that, as opposed to the findings of two previous highly regarded studies which relied predominantly on roll-call vote analysis to investigate the effects of race on the representation of black interests (Swain 1993; Whitby 1997), the results here show that, when agenda-setting behavior (i.e., bill introductions) is examined, a legislator's race tends to have a stronger effect on substantive representation than does a legislator's party membership.[18] The data in table 2.8 also indicate that districts with a majority black population had no significant impact on whether legislators representing such districts introduced black interest legislation. Moreover, the percentage of blacks in legislative districts had a significant positive effect on bill introductions in only one of the five categories of black interests legislation: civil rights issues.

Given that traditional civil rights issues have historically been and remain among the most prominent black interest areas, it is noteworthy that the presence of African Americans in legislative districts seems to influence the bill introduction behavior of representatives on these matters. Today, however, as we move into the twenty-first century, education, health, and social welfare issues are arguably just as important, if not more so, for the well-being and advancement of African Americans. In fact, one could argue that most traditional civil rights challenges like voting rights, fair and equal access to housing and public accommodations, and antidiscrimination legislation have for the most part been met. The percentage of blacks in the district had no significant impact on the propensity of a representative to place bills in these other important black interest areas (i.e., education, health, and social welfare) on the legislative and policy agendas. In these instances, the race of legislators appears to be a more important factor in black interest representation than the racial makeup of legislative districts. This suggests that there is indeed a connection between how legislatures look (descriptive representation) and what they produce (substantive representation).

CONCLUSION

The central question in this chapter asked whether African American representatives in state legislatures have behaved, as has been widely expected, like race representatives in their bill introduction and agenda-setting behavior. Race representatives are those women and men who assume leadership positions, either elected or unelected, in the African American community, and whose main objective is to advance the interests of black citizens. In political institutions like legislatures, race representatives seek to insure that a black perspective is articulated, understood, and advanced.

Relying on data from five state legislatures and three legislative sessions, the analyses here yield significant evidence that African American legislators do indeed behave as race representatives in their agenda-setting behavior. In each of the legislative sessions studied, a majority of the African American legislators introduced black interest bills. In contrast, in only one instance did the total number of nonblack representatives to do so exceed 25 percent. Also, of all the bills that African American legislators collectively introduced, the proportion that they devoted to black interests was greater than the proportion that their white counterparts devoted to these issues. Moreover, African Americans were twice as likely as nonblacks to introduce this type of legislation in the first place.

TABLE 2.8
EFFECTS OF RACE ON BILL INTRODUCTIONS

Independent Variable	Parameter Estimates (Standard Errors in Parentheses)					
	Black Interests	Women's Interests	Education Policy	Health Care	Children's Policy	Welfare Policy
Intercept	-3.82**	-3.21**	1.44**	-.474**	-2.50**	-1.19**
	(.53)	(.34)	(.22)	(.18)	(.27)	(.33)
Race	2.06**	.66**	.28*	-.08	.09	.39*
	(.21)	(.22)	(.15)	(.14)	(.20)	(.18)
Gender	.45*	1.51**	.18**	.31**	.53**	.32**
	(.21)	(.12)	(.08)	(.08)	(.11)	(.13)
Black woman	-.86*	-.62*	-.24	-.13	.14	-.08
	(.52)	(.35)	(.23)	(.30)	(.31)	(.29)
Republican	-.71**	.13	-.05	-.11*	-.19*	-.36**
	(.14)	(.09)	(.05)	(.05)	(.01)	(.08)
Seniority	.01	-.01	.02**	.01**	-.02**	.01
	(.01)	(.01)	(.00)	(.00)	(.01)	(.01)
% Black in district (logged)	.07*	.08**	-.00	.02	.00	.04
	(.04)	(.03)	(.02)	(.12)	(.03)	(.03)
Majority black district	.65	.22	-.11	-.09	-.41	.18
	(.47)	(.40)	(.18)	(.23)	(.37)	(.33)
Size of largest city (logged)	.15**	.08**	-.06**	.05**	.11**	.07**
	(.05)	(.03)	(.02)	(.01)	(.02)	(.02)
Largest city and Majority black district	-.41	-.24	-.00	.18	.14	.28
	(.49)	(.45)	(.22)	(.24)	(.38)	(.37)

Membership on relevant committee	.20	.19**	.75**	.56**	.21**	.43**
	(.13)	(.08)	(.05)	(.05)	(.08)	(.09)
No. of other bills introduced	.02**	.02**	.02**	.02**	.02**	.01**
	(.00)	(.00)	(.00)	(.00)	(.00)	(.00)
Arkansas	.01	-.27	-.35**	-.65**	-.23	-.66**
	(.25)	(.18)	(.09)	(.11)	(.15)	(.19)
Illinois	-.16	.37**	.09	-.32**	-.05	.10
	(.22)	(.15)	(.08)	(.09)	(.14)	(.13)
Maryland	-1.2**	.64**	-.30	-.18*	.58**	.04
	(.26)	(.146)	(.08)	(.09)	(.14)	(.13)
New Jersey	-.48*	.52**	.25**	.04	.55**	.69**
	(.25)	(.17)	(.09)	(.09)	(.15)	(.14)
North Carolina	.55**	-.29*	-.11	-.41**	.03	-1.0**
	(.25)	(.17)	(.09)	(.09)	(.15)	(.17)
1979	-1.1**	.55**	-.80**	.22**	.13	-.43**
	(.18)	(.11)	(.06)	(.06)	(.09)	(.09)
1989	-.18	.74**	-.35**	.50**	.95**	-.02
	(.17)	(.11)	(.06)	(.06)	(.09)	(.09)
Total number of bills	284	733	3,028	3,715	1,179	1,159

Source: Bratton and Haynie 1999a: 668–69.

Notes: Dependent Variable = number of bills a legislator introduced in a category.

Number of cases = 2,023

**$p \leq .01$ (one-tailed test)

*$p \leq .05$ (one-tailed test)

While it is clear that the African American state legislators from the five states included in this study were the primary advocates for black interests within their respective legislatures, it is also the case that these representatives did not focus exclusively on race matters. In fact, black interest legislation made up a majority of the bills that African American legislators introduced in only two of fourteen legislative sessions (tables 2.6 and 2.7). This finding provides evidence and reasons for us to consider these African American state legislators as characteristic of David Canon's "balancing perspective." With the balancing perspective, black legislators may make special efforts to articulate and pursue a race-based or race-related set of issues, but they also devote some time to working on legislative issues that have no race-specific content (Canon 1999:47–49). In the final analysis, when it comes to substantive representation, we can say with some significant degree of certainty that when African Americans are present in the legislature, they are more likely to pursue black interests than their nonblack counterparts.

In light of these findings, the speculation by Charles Bullock (1975) that I included at the beginning of this chapter merits repeating. Bullock suggested that it is possible that "well-meaning white politicians may be unable to comprehend some black needs and therefore fail to introduce them into the policy-making arena. Consequently, adequate representation of black demands . . . requires that there be black officeholders to translate these demands into policy" (727). Because assessing the motives of white legislators is beyond the scope of this study, I am not in a position to comment on their intentions relative to black interests. However, consistent with Bullock's conjecture, the evidence here indicates that there is an important link between descriptive and substantive representation. The race of the representative is linked to the kind of responsiveness African American citizens get from legislative institutions. This finding of a powerful and significant connection between descriptive and substantive representation is particularly noteworthy in light of the mounting theoretical, legal, and political challenges to the creation of majority-minority or minority-influence legislative districts—the type of districts from which most African American legislators are elected.

Miller v. Johnson (1995) and *Bush v. Vera* (1996) are just two examples of relatively recent U.S. Supreme Court decisions that exemplify the political and legal challenges to majority-minority districts.[19] The Court ruled in *Miller* that states could consider race in redistricting decisions, but race could not be the "predominant factor." In *Bush* the Supreme Court reaffirmed its decision in *Miller* by finding three majority-minority districts in Texas to be unconstitutional because race was the predominant factor used in drawing the district boundaries. Supreme Court decisions such as these are likely to lead to a decrease or, at the very least, stagnation in the number of African Americans elected to legislatures. If this is indeed the outcome, given my findings above, a likely consequence will be less substantive representation of black interests in important political institutions like state legislatures.

In her landmark 1993 book, *Black Faces, Black Interests: The Representation of African Americans in Congress,* Carol Swain provides one of the most compelling theoretical challenges to the purposeful drawing of districts specifically designed to elect a racial or ethnic minority. She argues that the presence of African Americans is not a prerequisite for the adequate (i.e., substantive) representation of black interests. Comparing the roll-call behavior of African American members of the 100th Congress to white members who represented significant numbers of black constituents, Swain concludes: "Descriptive representation of blacks guarantees only black faces and is, at best, an intangible good; substantive representation is by definition real and color blind. . . . Many white members of Congress perform as well or better on the indicators used in this book than some black representatives" (Swain 1993:211). To this she adds:

> What difference does the race of the representative make for the representation of black policy preferences? If the mean interest-group scores of white and black Democrats on two of the indicators of black interests are contrasted, there is only a shade of difference between white and black Democrats. . . . Similarly, in a multivariate regression analysis that includes the race of the representative as one of the independent variables, race is statistically insignificant. (Swain 1993:212).

These conclusions are clearly challenged by the data and analyses presented in this chapter. With regards to agenda-setting, an extremely important legislative function, I find that there is indeed a connection between the presence of African Americans in legislatures and the substantive representation of black interests.[20] The data and analyses here show that black state legislators are the primary advocates for black interests. For example, African American representatives, all else being equal, are significantly more likely than nonblack legislators to introduce bills that prohibit racial discrimination in employment and housing, and laws that advance the educational and social welfare interests of black citizens. Moreover, these analyses indicate that for the substantive representation of African American interests, a legislator's race matters above and beyond the effects of constituency characteristics and political party membership. In other words, black faces in legislatures *do* matter for black interest representation. Thus while super-majority black legislative districts in and of themselves may not be necessary to achieve substantive representation of black interests, they are important precisely because African American representatives are significantly more likely to be elected from such districts.

Several relatively recent studies on race and representation in the U.S. Congress have reached conclusions about the link between descriptive and substantive representation that are consistent with the ones reached here (Cameron, Epstein, and O'Halloran 1996; Canon 1995, 1999; Grofman, Griffin, and Glazer 1992; Lublin 1997; Whitby 1997). For example, Whitby, in his book *The Color of Representation: Congressional Behavior and Black Interests,* finds that the race of the representative indeed matters and is a significant predictor of responsiveness to black interests, and that race is an important factor even when controlling for the strong impact of party and region (Whitby 1997:109).

> The findings presented here have potentially important political consequences. There is more to the election of African Americans than symbolism or the color of skin. *The color of Congress has implications for the quality of substantive representation for African Americans.* The high level of support among black lawmakers is unmatched by any other cohort in the assembly.
> (Whitby 1997:112; emphasis added)

Similarly, Canon's book, *Race, Redistricting, and Representation: The Unintended Consequences of Black Majority Districts,* finds that African American legislators have distinctive representational styles that matter. Canon concludes that

> African American members of the House *are* more attentive to the distinctive needs of the black constituents than are their white counterparts who represent substantial numbers of blacks. . . . *The race of the representative has important implications for the type of representation that is provided to a district with a significant number of black constituents.* Black members do a better job walking the racial tightrope and balancing the distinctive needs of black voters and the general interests of all voters, black and white alike. White members tend to have a more exclusive focus on nonracial issues.
> (Canon 1999:244–45; italics in the original)

The findings of these two books and those from this chapter have important implications for legislative redistricting and for the procedures that we use to choose our elected representatives. If it is in fact true that African American representatives are the primary and most important advocates and supporters of black interests, then it is essential that efforts are undertaken to increase, enhance, and sustain African American representation in state legislatures, as well as in other policy-making arenas. Failure to do so runs the risk of not only once again excluding African Americans from a physical and descriptive presence in American political institutions; it is likely to diminish substantive governmental responsiveness to their concerns as well.

CHAPTER 3

RACE, REPRESENTATION, AND COMMITTEE ASSIGNMENTS

Legislative scholars have long recognized that standing committees are central to the legislative process.[1] Standing committees are significant for both the policy-making process and the career paths of legislators. There are two important policy-making functions that committees perform. One is the division of labor. Given the large volume and often technical complexity of legislation, committees provide a system of specialization that allows legislatures to make educated and informed choices (Shepsle 1975, 1988; Stewart 1992). Second, standing committees play an agenda-setting and gatekeeping role for legislatures. Committees not only control the substantive content of bills, they also determine if and when a piece of legislation will reach the full legislature. They have the capacity to prevent legislation—even that which might enjoy the support of the majority of the legislature—from ever being considered. In so doing, committees can substantially control the sets of issues and policy initiatives that are debated and decided in legislatures (Hall 1987; Rosenthal 1974; Smith and Deering 1984).

As for legislative careers, the committee assignments that a legislator receives can significantly influence that member's reelection chances. Legislators tend to seek membership on committees that are relevant to the interests found in their districts. Such assignments allow representatives to act or appear to act in a manner that is responsive to his or her constituents (Eulau and

Karps 1977; Fenno 1973; Rhode and Shepsle 1973; Stewart 1992). Committee assignments also enable legislators to pursue their personal interests, and they can help enhance a representative's position or status within the institution (Hibbing 1991; Munger 1988; Shepsle 1988).

Along with the central roles they play in the legislative process and in enhancing members' careers, committee assignments also have instrumental importance. It is through their participation in committees that legislators have their greatest direct effect on public policy. From the representative's perspective, however, all committee assignments are not the same. Committees have varying jurisdictions and unique responsibilities, and legislators are better able to have their own policy agendas advanced if they receive certain committee assignments rather than others (Bratton and Haynie 1999b; Francis 1989; Rhode and Shepsle 1973; Stewart 1992). As a result, legislators view some committee assignments as more desirable.

In chapter 2, I focused on the impact that African American state legislators have on the legislative process by examining their agenda-setting behavior. In this chapter the focus remains the same, but here I examine the African American representatives' standing committee assignment patterns rather than their bill introductions. Given the central role that committees play in legislatures, an examination of committee assignments provides us another appropriate opportunity to evaluate how African American legislators influence the policy-making process.

Kenneth Shepsle (1988) has suggested that because standing committees are jurisdictionally based, their members acquire an important stake in their respective jurisdictions. He argues that, as a consequence, committees

> are not legislatures writ small; they are not representative of the larger legislature. To the contrary, they are highly unrepresentative, consisting mainly of "interesteds" or "preference outliers." . . . It suits legislators fine, because this arrangement permits them to specialize and accumulate power in just those areas that are of special interest to those who must renew their contracts every other year.   (Shepsle 1988:471–72)

Because of this characteristic (i.e., consisting mainly of "interesteds" and "preference outliers"), standing committees also provide another excellent venue from which to explore whether or not, and to what degree, African American state legislators behave like race representatives. We know from chapter 2 that black interests and matters of race are of special concern to race representatives. Therefore, if African American legislators do indeed behave as race representatives, we can expect them to allocate a significant share of their committee assignments to committees whose jurisdictions include black interest issues.

THE COMMITTEE ASSIGNMENT PROCESS

Accommodating members' requests appears to be the norm in the committee assignment process in state legislatures. This norm of accommodation is in part a consequence of attempts of party leaders to achieve and maintain party unity by creating a satisfying work environment for their members (Hedlund 1989). The lack of a strong and entrenched seniority system in state legislatures contributes to this norm by providing party leaders and legislative officers with more flexibility in meeting members' request (Francis 1989; Rosenthal 1981).

As evidence of this tendency toward accommodation, Wayne Francis (1989) cites a 1981 Council of State Governments national survey in which 83.4 percent of responding state legislators indicated that they were "pleased" with their standing committee assignments. Similarly, James Button and David Hedge (1993), in a 1991–92 national survey of state lawmakers, found that 92 percent of all responding legislators reported that they were either "satisfied" or "very satisfied" with their committee assignments. Other legislative committees studies, conducted at both the congressional and state legislative levels, provide additional persuasive evidence that comports with the results of these surveys, which illustrate that legislators' committee assignment requests tend to be accommodated by legislative and party leaders (Bullock 1985; Gertzog 1976; Hedlund 1989, 1992; Shepsle 1978).[2]

INTEREST REPRESENTATION AND COMMITTEE ASSIGNMENTS

One of the consequences of this norm of accommodation has been for legislators to sort themselves out on committees based on their personal or district interests. Francis (1989) argues that because of this we can expect, in general, that

there will be an abundance of requests for a small number of powerful standing committees, almost always including those dealing with appropriations, taxation, or budgeting; but beyond the prime committees, interests will be scattered, suited to personal background and constituency make-up.

(27)

We know from the previous literature on legislative committees that the desire to represent one's district is one of the most important reasons for legislators' seeking membership on particular committees (e.g., Bullock 1973; Eulau and Karps 1977; Fenno 1973; Rhode and Shepsle 1973; Stewart 1992). We also know that committees provide members with an important strategic position from which to promote and advance their policy agendas. And, given that the overwhelming majority of African American legislators are elected from majority black districts with distinctive needs, the expectation is that African American legislators will seek and hold assignments on those committees whose jurisdictions include black interest policy areas. That is, we should expect to find African Americans significantly represented on committees whose jurisdiction includes health, social welfare, education, civil rights, and employment opportunity issues.[3] This pattern should be more pronounced in the earlier session (i.e., 1969), when African American representation in state legislatures was still fairly new and when there was heightened awareness of the social and economic conditions of the African American community following the 1960s civil rights movement.[4]

The difficulty of satisfactorily characterizing what, in fact, district or constituency interests are is a major problem found in much of the scholarly literature that attempts to link legislators' committee assignment preferences to district interests. Eulau (1985), for example, has asserted that researchers often inappropriately substitute measures of regional or state interest for district or constituency interests.[5] Because of this seeming inability to find appropriate measures of constituency interest, Eulau argues that "'representation' in any other than its descriptive-statistical sense seems to have little purchasing power in the committee assignment studies" (Eulau 1985:212). Notwithstanding this sound and persuasive critique, with regards to the representation of black interests, I believe that identifying the interests of African American constituents and connecting them to committees in legislatures is not as harrowing an undertaking nor even the nearly impossible task that Eulau suggests it might be.

Given a shared cultural background and common historical heritage, and given the fact that African Americans have been one of the most stable and consistent groups on questions of public policy and political ideology (Dawson 1994; Gurin, Hatchett, and Jackson 1989), it is indeed possible both to speak in terms of and identify a black constituency with particular interests. For instance, the Congressional Black Caucus (CBC) in the U.S. Congress, since its inception in 1971, has seen itself as representing "the national Black Community" (Barnett 1975). This conception of a national African American community rests on the notion of a "commonality of black political interests" and on the belief that African American members of Congress can and should "jointly represent" this "black collectivity" (Barnett 1975:38). Making a similar point, Canon (1999) writes, "The formative political experiences for the founding members of the CBC were in the civil rights movement of the 1960s. . . . Many members saw themselves as the spokespersons for all African Americans, not only those in their congressional districts" (40). At the state level, in a study of the North Carolina Legislative Black Caucus, Cheryl Miller (1990) concluded that "the Caucus was emerging in its own mind, as well as in the minds of the General Assembly, media, and other political actors, as being an effective voice for minority concerns" (343).

Thus, while in theory the political actions of persons serving in state legislatures should be governed first by a desire to represent not a state or a region but a particular district within a state, African American legislators are often faced with or undertake the additional obligation of pursuing racial group representation. That is, the political behavior of black legislators is often governed by a desire and effort to represent both their individual district *and* African American citizens, regardless of where the citizens reside.[6] Therefore, connecting the standing committee assignments of African American legislators to their attempts to substantively represent black interests and African American constituencies is more defensible theoretically and more easily done empirically than the attempts criticized by Eulau.

DATA AND METHODS

The data analyzed here consist of the standing committee assignments from the lower legislative chamber of the Arkansas, Illinois, Maryland, New Jersey, and North Carolina legislatures for 1969, 1979, and 1989. These data were collected from the various state legislative manuals and legislative journals. With the exception of black interest committees, only those committees on which an African American legislator served in at least one of the three legislative sessions are included in the analyses. Using this criteria, the number of committees analyzed ranges from seven in Maryland to twenty-six in Illinois. State legislative committees often undergo name changes. However, here, if a committee's name changed but its jurisdiction remained the same, only the original name appears in the tables that follow.

The primary task in this chapter is to examine the standing committee assignment patterns of African American legislators. This examination is intended to shed some additional light on black representatives' impact on the legislative process. It will also allow us to further investigate the extent to which African American legislators behave as race representatives. I use two measures—saliency and influence potential—to assess African American representation on legislative committees.

Committee jurisdictions rarely are stagnant or have concretely defined boundaries. In fact, various committees often have jurisdictions that overlap. Thus it is possible for legislators to use more than one committee to accomplish their representational goals. Because of this, it is difficult to infer conclusively exactly what legislators' presence on or absence from a particular committee means (Canon 1999). Nevertheless, the two representational measures used here can provide some relevant information that allows us to reasonably estimate the significance and instrumental value of particular standing committee assignments to African American legislators and their policy agendas, especially as they pertain to black interests.

The first measure, *saliency,* operationalized as the percentage of the total number of all African American committee assignments devoted to a particular committee, provides an assessment of the relative importance of that committee and the policy areas within its jurisdiction to black legislators.[7] For example, in a legislative session in which African American legislators held a total of ten committee assignments, and four of those assignments were on the Education Committee, the Education Committee would have a saliency score of 40 percent; and if two of those assignments were on the Transportation Committee, then the Transportation Committee's saliency score would be 20 percent. We could then say that, based on their committee service, education issues resonated more with African American legislators than did transportation issues.

The second measure that I use, referred to here as *influence potential,* is a commonly used measure: the percentage of a committee's members who are African American. Because committees enable their members to specialize and acquire power in the policy areas within their jurisdiction, the degree to which a cohesive well-organized group is represented on a committee reflects that group's potential influence over certain policy areas.

As I use them here, an implicit assumption of both of these measures is that there was some strategic consultation among the African American legislators in each state regarding the allocation of their standing committee assignments. While substantiating that such consultations actually took place is beyond the scope of this study, there is evidence in the existing literature that suggests that this type of decision-making is not uncommon among black legislative caucuses. For example, in her study of agenda-setting activities of the North Carolina Legislative Black Caucus, Cheryl Miller (1990:12) found that African American legislators strategically used their dispersion and leadership on various committees in order to improve the probability of passage of their priority legislation. Similarly, David Canon (1995, 1999) reports that the Congressional Black Caucus has long had an explicit goal of having at least one of its members on each of the most important standing committees. All five of the states in this study had formal legislative black caucuses in at least one of the relevant legislative sessions.

SALIENCY AND AFRICAN AMERICAN COMMITTEE ASSIGNMENTS

Table 3.1 provides information on how salient black legislators found the various types of committees in each of the five states and for all three of the legislative sessions included in this study. From these data we see that black interest committees—those committees whose jurisdictions include black interest policy areas like health, education, civil rights, and social welfare—were extremely prominent assignments among African American representatives. (Black interest committees are presented in tables 3.2, 3.3, 3.4, 3.5, and 3.6.) Because state legislatures vary in the number of standing committees they have, and because committee jurisdictions often differ from legislative session to legislative session and from state to state, the number and particular committees that are classified as black interest committees will be different from state to state and/or from session to session. Appendix 1 contains a list of all the committees classified by committee type for each of the five states.

The saliency of black interest committees to black legislators ranged from 23 percent in Illinois (1979) to 60 percent in New Jersey (1989). In eleven of the fourteen cases, assignments on black interest committees were ranked at the top in terms of their saliency to African American representatives. This suggests that in deciding on which standing committees to serve, the black legislators acted in a manner that is consistent with what we would expect of race

TABLE 3.1

SALIENCY AND AFRICAN AMERICAN REPRESENTATION ON HOUSE
STANDING COMMITTEES IN THE FIVE STATES, BY COMMITTEE TYPE
(1969, 1979, AND 1989)

State/Committee Type**	Saliency*		
	1969	1979	1989
Arkansas			
Black interests	—	42.9	25.0
Constituency	—	14.3	31.3
Policy	—	0	6.3
Prestige	—	0	6.3
Miscellaneous	—	42.9	31.3
Illinois			
Black interests	45.7	22.9	23.9
Constituency	17.1	14.3	11.9
Policy	22.8	25.7	35.8
Prestige	8.6	28.6	17.9
Miscellaneous	5.7	8.6	14.9
Maryland			
Black interests	53.3	40.0	56.5
Constituency	20.0	6.7	4.0
Policy	0	26.7	21.7
Prestige	2.9	26.7	17.4
Miscellaneous	23.8	0	0
New Jersey			
Black interests	33.3	60.0	33.3
Constituency	0	0	0
Policy	16.7	20.0	16.7
Prestige	16.7	20.0	33.3
Miscellaneous	33.3	0	16.7
North Carolina			
Black interests	42.9	41.7	35.7
Constituency	0	0	0
Policy	28.6	25.0	7.1
Prestige	28.6	25.0	23.8
Miscellaneous	0	8.3	33.3

Saliency is the percentage of the total number of black committee assignments designated for that particular committee type.

**With the exception of the black interest committee, the committee types are from Smith and Deering (1990:87). Black interest committees are those committees whose jurisdiction includes such black interest policy areas as health, education, civil rights, and general social welfare. For example, Judiciary, Education and Health committees are classified as black interest rather than policy committees. See the appendix to chapter 3 for committee classifications for each state.

representatives. That is, their committee assignment decisions appear to have
been guided, at least in part, by a concern for addressing the particular needs
and interests of African American constituents.

As expected, assignments on black interest committees were generally more
salient in the earlier legislative session than in the latter one. Only in Maryland
did the saliency of black interest committees increase between 1969 and 1989. In
New Jersey, saliency on these committees was the same in 1989 as it was in 1969.
There are several possible explanations for this pattern of African American
legislators' allocating fewer of their committee slots to black interest committees over time. One possibility for this trend is that it reflects the overall improvements in the political and socioeconomic status of African Americans as
a group over the last two and a half to three decades.

Notwithstanding the fact that serious social and economic problems continue to plague the African American community and that African Americans
continue to be less well-off economically relative to white Americans (Dewart
1990; Hacker 1992; Massey and Denton 1993; Tidwell 1992; Wilson 1987), it is
also the case that, in many respects, there has been tremendous progress. In areas such as educational achievement, white-collar employment, and home
ownership, the number and percentage of African Americans in the middle
class have all generally followed a steep upward trend since 1960 (Canon 1999;
Thernstrom and Thernstrom 1997). Also, most of the political goals of the civil
rights movement, such as the protection of voting rights and ending de jure
discrimination and segregation, have been accomplished. And in many respects, there is less national or widespread attention given to these issues. It is
possible that these improvements have resulted in a shift in focus or priorities,
or even a broadening of the conceptualization of black interests on the part of
African American representatives. That is, perhaps in the minds and behavior
of black legislators, how black interests are now conceived entails placing more
emphasis and direct attention on issues such as commerce and economic policy, business entrepreneurship, community development, and environmental
quality, and less on government-provided social programs and traditional civil
rights issues (Whitby 1987).

Efforts to advance their legislative careers and efforts to become more incorporated into the "mainstream" of the legislative institution are two additional potential explanations for the apparent decline in the saliency of black
interest committee assignments to African American legislators. Obtaining
seats on those committees deemed to be the most prestigious in the legislature
is an important vehicle for accomplishing both of these outcomes.[8] Typically,

the Appropriations, Budget, Finance, Taxation, and Rules committees are considered to be the most prestigious in a legislature (Francis 1989). Not only are a
representative's chances of moving into leadership positions significantly en-
hanced by serving on one of these committees (Francis 1989; Rhode and Shepsle 1973; Shepsle 1975), his or her perceived or actual power, influence, and effectiveness within the institution may also depend on having such committee
assignments (Frantzich 1979; Friedman 1996; Meyer 1980; Weissert 1989). In
choosing their committees, African American legislators may find it difficult to
attend to the interests of their African American constituents while at the same
time they are attempting to improve their relative standing in the legislature
and advance their legislative careers (Friedman 1993). Consequently, there
might be some trade-off effect at work. That the saliency of prestige committee
assignments grew from 1969 to 1989 in three of the five states, while the saliency of black interest committees either stayed the same or declined during the
same period (table 3.1) is some evidence in support of this proposition.

Finally, this decline in the saliency of black interest committee assignments
might be evidence of the emergence of a different generation or a new type of
African American representative. This new generation of African American
representatives may be less inclined (or perhaps perceive less of a need) to be
the type of race representatives that their predecessors were. Canon (1995, 1999)
finds evidence of such a generation of black representatives emerging in the
U.S. Congress. He refers to them as products of the "politics of commonality."
Commonality representatives tend to be professional politicians whose formative political experiences were honed in elected office rather than the civil
rights movement.[9] They de-emphasize race and the racial aspects of political
issues in their legislative behavior. In other words, their general approach to
politics is based on multiracial or nonracial terms. They tend to seek to balance
their advocacy for black interests with concern for broader issues (Canon
1995:162–63; 1999:38–42). Given these characteristics, commonality-type legislators can be expected to have fewer black interest committee assignments than
"difference members."[10] They will tend to seek assignments on a variety of
committees whose jurisdictions extend beyond black interests. Canon's examination of this hypothesis using data from the 103rd and 104th U.S. congresses
yielded inconclusive results. As expected, the commonality members held fewer black interest committee assignments than difference members, but the differences were not statistically significant (1999:184).

An individual-level analysis like the one employed by Canon is not possible
with the data used for this study. Therefore I cannot determine whether Afri-

can Americans in the state legislatures can be reasonably divided into categories like "commonality" and "difference" members. Nevertheless, the findings in table 3.1 do demonstrate that, although black interest committees remained very popular throughout the period studied, the African American
legislators became more varied in rationing their committee assignments over
time. As was the case with their bill introductions, they seem to adopt what
Canon (1999) refers to as a "balancing perspective" in choosing their committee assignments.

AFRICAN AMERICAN COMMITTEE ASSIGNMENTS AND POLICY INFLUENCE POTENTIAL

Because they are jurisdictionally based and composed of members who are especially interested in the policy areas within their jurisdiction, standing committees generate agenda-setting and gatekeeping powers. Committee members
are empowered with substantial authority over policy-making in their committee's jurisdictions (Shepsle 1988). One consequence of this is that well-organized
and cohesive subgroups within a legislature, if they can amass significant representation on a given committee or set of committees, can strategically place
themselves to potentially exert noticeable and disproportionate influence over
specific issues or entire policy domains.

African American legislators form one such legislative subgroup. While it is
interesting and important to know which committees—and therefore which
issues—resonate the most (i.e., are more salient) with black state legislators, it
is perhaps more important to determine over which issues or jurisdictions they
have the most influence. Of particular concern here is their potential influence
over black interest matters. To make these determinations, I compare standing
committees in terms of their African American representation. The comparisons are made separately for each of the five states. Influence potential is measured as the percentage of a committee's members who are African American.[11] I also include an *equity ratio* measure for each committee, which assesses
the proportionality of African American representation on the committee. The
equity ratio is operationalized as the percentage of African Americans on the
committee *minus* the percentage of African Americans in the House. If, for example, African Americans constituted 15 percent of the Appropriations Committee and they made up 10 percent of the entire House, then the equity ratio
for this committee would be

> *% Appropriation Committee seats held by African Americans – % African*
> *Americans in the House*
> or .15 – .10 = .05

An equity ratio of 0 equals perfect proportional committee representation. A positive score indicates that African Americans are overrepresented on the committee, and a negative ratio means that they are underrepresented. Again, with the exception of black interest committees, only those committees on which an African American legislator served in at least one of the three legislative sessions are included in the analyses.

ARKANSAS

During the 1979 legislative session, African American legislators in Arkansas served on a total of six different standing committees; in 1989 they served on ten (table 3.2).[12] In both sessions they were represented on all the existing black interest committees except the Public Health, Welfare, and Labor Committee. Also in both sessions, at least one black interest committee was among the committees on which African Americans had the most potential influence— the Education Committee in both 1979 and 1989, and the Joint Committee on Children and Youth in 1989.

From the equity ratios in table 3.2, we see that on six committees in 1979 and four in 1989, the black legislator's representation exceeded their representation in the House. In both sessions, African Americans were, in general, the most overrepresented on black interest committees. For the period studied, the Judiciary Committee in 1989 is the only black interest committee on which African Americans in the Arkansas House were underrepresented. Besides black interest committees, African Americans' greatest potential for influence on public policy came on the Legislative Affairs and House Management committees.

ILLINOIS

In each of the three legislative sessions in Illinois, a black interest committee was the committee on which blacks exerted the greatest influence—the Public Welfare and Human Resources Committee in 1969, the Cities and Villages Committee in 1979, and the Urban Affairs Committee in 1989 (table 3.3).[13] African Americans were particularly well-placed to have an effect on social welfare policy in 1969, urban affairs in 1979, and on both categories in 1989. Moreover, in 1969, black representation on the Public Welfare and Human Resources

TABLE 3.2

AFRICAN AMERICAN REPRESENTATION ON ARKANSAS HOUSE STANDING COMMITTEES (1979 AND 1989)

Committee Name	1979 (N = 3)		1989 (N = 5)		Rank	
	% Black	Equity Ratio	% Black	Equity Ratio	1979	1989
City, County and Local Affairs	0	–3.0	5.0	0	—	T5
Joint Committee on Children and Youth	NE	NE	**20.0**	**15.0**	NE	1
Economic and Industrial Resources, and Development	9.6	6.0	NE	NE	3	NE
Education	**10.0**	**7.0**	**10.0**	**5.0**	T1	T2
House Management	5.0	.20	10.0	5.0	T4	T2
Insurance and Commerce	5.0	.20	5.0	0	T4	T5
Judiciary	**5.0**	**2.0**	**5.0**	**0**	T4	T5
Legislative Affairs	10.0	7.0	10.0	5.0	T1	T2
Public Health, Welfare, and Labor	**0**	**–3.0**	**0**	**–5.0**	—	T5
Public Transportation	0	–3.0	5.0	0	—	T5
Revenue and Taxation	*0*	*–3.0*	*5.0*	*0*	—	T5
State Agencies and Government Affairs	0	–3.0	5.0	0	—	T5

Notes: N = number of African Americans in the House.

NE = the committee was not in existence during that session.

Black interest committees appear in bold, prestige committees in italics. With the exception of black interest committees, only those committees in which an African American legislator served in one of the two sessions are included. No African Americans served in the House in 1969. The equity ratio is the percent of African Americans on the committee minus the percent of African Americans in the House.

TABLE 3.3

AFRICAN AMERICAN REPRESENTATION ON *ILLINOIS* HOUSE STANDING COMMITTEES (1969, 1979, AND 1989)

Committee Name	1969 (N = 14)		1979 (N = 14)		1989 (N = 14)		Rank		
	% Black	Equity Ratio	% Black	Equity Ratio	% Black	Equity Ratio	1969	1979	1989
Appropriations	3.6	–4.3	7.7	–0.7	16.7	5.0	15	10	T6
Banks and Savings & Loans	11.1	3.2	4.2	–4.2	14.3	2.6	7	16	T9
Cities and Villages	NE	NE	21.4	13.0	0	–8.4	NE	1	—
Conservation and Water	5.9	–2.0	NE	NE	NE	NE	14	NE	NE
Consumer Protection	NE	NE	NE	NE	21.5	9.8	NE	NE	4
Contingent Expenses	20.0	12.1	NE	NE	NE	NE	2	NE	NE
County and Township Affairs	11.8	3.9	6.7	–1.7	7.7	–4.0	T4	T11	T17
Education	14.3	6.4	0	–7.9	13.3	1.6	3	0	11
Elections	10.7	2.8	15.0	6.6	7.7	–4.0	T8	T3	T17
Environment, Energy, and Natural Resources	NE	NE	6.7	–1.7	23.1	11.4	NE	T11	3
Executive	7.4	–0.5	10.5	2.1	14.3	2.6	11	T6	T9
Higher Education	0	–7.9	13.3	4.9	11.6	–0.6	—	5	14
Highways and Traffic Safety	0	–7.9	4.8	–3.6	8.0	–3.7	—	T14	16
Insurance	14.8	3.9	10.5	2.1	28.5	16.8	T4	T6	2

Judiciary	10.7	2.8	0	-8.4	10.0	-1.7	T8	—	15
Labor and Commerce	0	-7.9	6.7	-1.7	12.5	0.8	—	T11	T12
Municipalities	10.7	2.8	NE	NE	NE	NE	T8	NE	NE
Personnel and Pensions	NE	NE	20.0	11.6	0	-8.4	NE	2	—
Public Utilities	11.8	3.9	0	-8.4	15.5	3.8	T4	—	8
Public Welfare and Human Resources	**27.8**	**19.9**	**15.6**	**6.6**	**21.1**	**9.4**	**1**	**T3**	**5**
Registration and Regulation	6.3	-1.6	NE	NE	12.0	0.3	13	NE	14
Revenue	*0*	*-7.9*	*8.3*	*-0.1*	*12.5*	*0.8*	*13*	*NE*	*14*
Rules	*7.1*	*0.8*	*8.3*	*-0.1*	*6.3*	*-5.4*	*12*	*NE*	*19*
State Government	NE	NE	0	-8.4	16.7	5.0	NE	—	T6
Urban Affairs	**NE**	**NE**	**NE**	**NE**	**40.0**	**28.0**	**NE**	**NE**	**1**
Veterans Affairs	0	-7.9	4.8	-3.6	NE	NE	—	T14	NE

Notes: N = number of African Americans in the legislature.

NE = the committee was not in existence during that session.

Black interest committees appear in bold, prestige committees in italics. With the exception of black interest committees, only those committees in which an African American legislator served in one of the three sessions are included. The equity ratio is the percent of African Americans on the committee minus the percent of African Americans in the House.

Committee was almost twice the proportion of blacks in the House; and black representation on the Urban Affairs Committee in 1989 was nearly three times the percentage of African Americans in the legislature.

The most noticeable trend in Illinois, however, is the declining African American presence on black interest committees over time. Every black interest committee that existed and had at least one black member in both 1969 and 1989 experienced a drop in African American representation. No blacks served on the Higher Education Committee in 1969, but between 1979 and 1989 black influence declined on this committee as well. In terms of the percentage of African American members, two of the top three committees in 1969, and three of the top four in 1979 were black interest committees. By 1989, however, only one of the top four committees with the highest proportion of black members was a black interest committee. This pattern is consistent with the committee saliency findings for Illinois (table 3.1). Over time, African American legislators clearly expanded their presence to committees that were not directly linked to black interests, like the Executive and Insurance committees.

MARYLAND

In the Maryland House of Delegates, as in Illinois, a black interest committee was the committee on which blacks exerted the greatest influence for each of the legislative sessions. The Constitutional and Administrative Law Committee was the highest-ranked committee in terms of the percentage of African Americans members in both 1969 and 1989 (table 3.4).[14] The Constitutional and Administrative Law Committee's jurisdiction includes election laws, workers' compensation, and amendments to the state constitution. In 1979 the Economic Matters Committee ranked first in African American representation. Unemployment insurance and consumer protection are among the areas covered by the Economic Matters Committee. It is somewhat surprising that African American legislators were consistently and significantly underrepresented on the Judiciary Committee throughout the period studied.

The representation of African Americans on all the black interest committees increased over time. In fact, on three of the four black interest committees, the African American presence more than doubled between 1969 and 1989. For example, in 1969 black legislators made up 12.5 percent of the Constitutional and Administrative Law Committee and 2.9 percent of the Economic Matters Committee. By 1989, African Americans constituted more than 27 percent of the total membership of the Constitutional and Administrative Law Commit-

TABLE 3.4

AFRICAN AMERICAN REPRESENTATION ON *MARYLAND* HOUSE STANDING COMMITTEES

(1969, 1979, AND 1989)

Committee Name	1969 (N = 8)		1979 (N = 14)		1989 (N = 22)		Rank		
	% Black	Equity Ratio	% Black	Equity Ratio	% Black	Equity Ratio	1969	1979	1989
Appropriations	*NE*	*NE*	*12.5*	*2.6*	*12.5*	*–3.1*	*NE*	*3*	*4*
Constitutional and Administrative Law	12.5	6.9	13.6	3.7	27.3	11.7	1	2	1
Economic Matters	2.9	–2.7	17.4	7.5	18.2	2.6	T4	1	2
Environmental Matters	7.4	1.8	4.2	–5.7	4.2	–11.4	3	7	7
Judiciary	2.9	–2.7	4.3	–5.6	8.7	–6.9	T4	6	5
Rules and Executive Nominations	*0*	*–5.6*	*6.7*	*–3.2*	*7.5*	*–8.1*	*—*	*5*	*6*
Ways and Means	11.1	5.5	8.3	–1.6	16.7	1.1	2	4	3

Notes: N = number of African Americans in the legislature.

NE = the committee was not in existence during that session.

Black interest committees appear in bold, prestige committees in italics. With the exception of black interest committees, only those committees in which an African American legislator served in one of the three sessions are included. The equity ratio is the percent of African Americans on the committee minus the percent of African Americans in the House.

tee, and slightly more than 18 percent of the Economic Matters Committee. This growth was contrary to what was predicted. Their presence on these committees as well as the Ways and Means Committee placed African American representatives in a position to have significant influence on the issues of particular importance to their African American constituents, such as election laws, unemployment insurance, education, and social welfare programs.

Black legislators in Maryland had a presence on at least one prestige committees in all the sessions. However, in four of the five instances, their representation on these committees was lower than their proportion in the legislature as a whole. The equity ratios also reveal that when the black legislators were overrepresented on a committee, it was almost always on a black interest committee. The only exceptions are the 1969 Environmental Matters Committee and the 1979 Appropriations Committee.

NEW JERSEY

The data in table 3.5 indicate that African American legislators in New Jersey tended to spread themselves out almost evenly across a relatively small number of committees. In 1969, for example, African American legislators served on only six of twenty-one committees that existed. In 1979 it was five out of seventeen, and in 1989 they served on only four of a possible twenty-two committees. Thus it appears that the representatives sought to narrowly target their areas of influence.

The black legislators maintained a presence on important black interest committees in each of the legislative sessions. They were overrepresented on the Education as well as Institutions and Welfare committees in 1969 and 1979, on the Judiciary Committee in 1979, and on the Housing Committee in 1989. It is interesting that no African American served on the Higher Education Committee in either of the three sessions.

NORTH CAROLINA

Black legislators in North Carolina tended to divide their standing committee assignments mostly between black interest and prestige committees (table 3.6). In 1969, of the seven committees that had African American representation, five of them fit this description, as did six of the nine in 1979 and seven of the fourteen in 1989. African Americans were overrepresented on at least one prestige committee in each of the legislative sessions. And, when one considers all the sessions together, on black interest committees they were overrepresented

TABLE 3.5

AFRICAN AMERICAN REPRESENTATION ON *NEW JERSEY* HOUSE STANDING COMMITTEES (1969, 1979, AND 1989)

Committee Name	1969 ($N=5$)		1979 ($N=3$)		1989 ($N=5$)		Rank		
	% Black	Equity Ratio	% Black	Equity Ratio	% Black	Equity Ratio	1969	1979	1989
Appropriations	*0*	*-6.3*	*0*	*-3.7*	*13.3*	*6.2*	—	—	*4*
Community Development and Urban Affairs	NE	NE	NE	NE	20.0	12.9	NE	NE	T1
County and Municipal Government	0	-6.3	14.3	10.6	0	-7.1	—	T4	—
Education	11.1	4.8	14.3	10.6	0	-7.1	T2	T4	—
Higher Education	0	-6.3	NE	NE	0	-7.1	—	—	—
Housing	NE	NE	NE	NE	20.0	12.9	NE	NE	T1
Institutions and Welfare	11.1	4.8	20.0	16.3	NE	NE	T2	T1	NE
Introduction of Bills	14.3	8.0	NE	NE	NE	NE	1	NE	NE
Judiciary	0	-6.3	20.0	16.3	0	-7.1	—	T1	—
State Government	0	-6.3	0	-3.7	20.0	12.9	—	—	T1
Taxation	*11.1*	*4.8*	*0*	*-3.7*	*NE*	*NE*	*T2*	—	*NE*
Transportation and Public Utilities	11.1	4.8	0	-3.7	0	-7.1	T2	—	—
Ways and Means	*0*	*-6.3*	*20.0*	*16.3*	*NE*	*NE*	—	*T1*	*NE*

Notes: N = number of African Americans in the legislature.

NE = the committee was not in existence during that session.

Black interest committees appear in bold, prestige committees in italics. With the exception of black interest committees, only those committees in which an African American legislator served in one of the three sessions are included. The equity ratio is the percent of African Americans on the committee minus the percent of African Americans in the House.

TABLE 3.6

AFRICAN AMERICAN REPRESENTATION ON *NORTH CAROLINA* HOUSE STANDING COMMITTEES

(1969, 1979, AND 1989)

Committee Name	1969 (N = 1)		1979 (N = 2)		1989 (N = 13)		Rank		
	% Black	Equity Ratio	% Black	Equity Ratio	% Black	Equity Ratio	1969	1979	1989
Alcoholic Beverage Control	0	-0.8	0	-1.7	28.6	17.8	—	—	T1
Appropriations	*1.6*	*0.8*	*1.6*	*-0.1*	*9.8*	*-1.0*	*7*	*9*	*11*
Banking and Banks	4.3	3.5	0	-1.7	0	-10.8	4	—	—
Budget	*NE*	*NE*	*5.3*	*3.6*	*NE*	*NE*	*NE*	*7*	*NE*
Constitutional Amendments	0	-0.8	10.5	8.8	NE	NE	—	2	NE
Correctional Institutions	8.3	7.5	0	-1.7	0	-10.8	1	—	—
Courts and Judicial Districts	0	-0.8	12.5	10.8	NE	NE	—	1	NE
Economy	0	-0.8	6.7	5.0	0	0	—	3	—
Education	3.7	2.9	0	-1.7	14.3	3.5	5	—	T5
Election Laws	0	-0.8	5.9	4.2	14.3	3.5	—	4	T5
Finance	*0*	*-0.8*	*1.7*	*0*	*7.8*	*-3.0*	*—*	*8*	*13*
Higher Education	0	-0.8	5.6	3.9	7.1	-3.7	—	T5	14
Judiciary (I, II, III)	4.5	3.7	5.6	3.9	13.8	3.0	3	T5	10
Military, Veteran, and Indian Affairs	0	-0.8	0	-1.7	14.3	3.5	—	—	T5

Pensions and Retirement	0	−0.8	0	−1.7	18.2	7.6	—	3
Public Employees	0	−0.8	0	−1.7	28.6	17.8	—	T1
Public Welfare	**3.1**	**2.3**	**0**	**−1.7**	**16.7**	**5.9**	6	4
Roads and Transportation	0	−0.8	0	−1.7	14.3	3.5	—	T5
Rules and Operation of the House	*5.3*	*4.5*	*0*	*−1.7*	*9.1*	*1.7*	*2*	*12*
State Government	0	−0.8	0	−1.7	14.3	3.5	—	T5
UNC Board of Governors	0	−0.8	0	−1.7	14.3	3.5	—	T5

Notes: N = number of African Americans in the legislature.

NE = the committee was not in existence during that session.

Black interest committees appear in bold, prestige committees in italics. With the exception of black interest committees, only those committees in which an African American legislator served in one of the three sessions are included. The equity ratio is the percent of African Americans on the committee minus the percent of African Americans in the House.

*The 1989 standing committee system was significantly different than in 1969 and 1979. By 1989, several committees that were previously stand-alone committees were now incorporated as subcommittees. For example, the Higher Education Committee became a subcommittee of the larger Education Committee, and Roads and Transportation became a subcommittee of the Infrastructure Committee. For the purposes of this analysis, where appropriate, such subcommittees were treated as full standing committees in order to maintain consistency and comparability.

in nine of thirteen cases. In no case, however, was a black interest committee ranked first in terms of the percentage of African Americans on it.

The 1989 committee representation pattern in North Carolina is similar to the one in Illinois in 1989. By 1989, while maintaining a significant presence on black interest committees, African American legislators in the North Carolina House had both expanded the number of committees on which they served and diversified the areas over which they had influence. The top three committees based on African American representation were committees whose jurisdictions were not directly linked to a black interest area, i.e. Alcoholic Beverage Control, Pensions and Retirement, and Public Employees. In the cases of the Alcoholic Beverage Control and the Public Employees committees, African American representation was at least more than one and a half times what it was on any black interest committee. The relatively high percentage of African Americans on these two committees may be explained, in part, by the fact that an African American legislator was part of the committees' leadership structure.

DISCUSSION

For all three of the legislative sessions in four of the five states, a black interest committee was among the top two committees in terms of the percentage of their members who were African American. Moreover, while they did not have representation on every possible black interest committee, if we consider all of the fourteen legislative sessions together, African Americans were overrepresented on thirty-nine of the forty-eight black interest committees on which they actually served. Thus, based on their standing committee assignments, African American legislators were in a position to specialize and accumulate power in those areas of particular importance to their African American constituents. That is, through their presence and participation on standing committees, African American legislators had the greatest potential to directly influence legislation in black interest categories.

Between 1969 and 1989, there was an increase in the number of committees on which black legislators served in three of the states—Arkansas, Illinois, and North Carolina. The number of committees on which African American legislators served in Maryland and New Jersey during this time stayed the same. Diversification in the substantive areas over which they had some influence accompanied this increase. For example, there were some indications that over time, the legislators increased their influence on prestige and internal house management committees. However, it does not appear that the African American legislators expanded their committee coverage at the expense of significantly lowering their influence on black interest committees. Only in Illinois was there a systematic decline in African American representation on black interest committees between 1969 and 1989. An increase in the number of African Americans elected to the legislatures was the most important factor driving the expanded committee coverage.

CONCLUSION

Standing committees play a central role in the legislative process. Because they can control the substantive content of legislation and determine if and when bills reach the floor, standing committees have tremendous control over the types of issues that are debated and decided in legislatures.

The desire to represent one's constituents and district is one of the most important considerations for legislators as they choose committee assignments (Bullock 1973; Eulau and Karps 1977; Francis 1989; Hedlund 1992; Rhode and Shepsle 1973; Stewart 1992). Because standing committees are jurisdictionally based, their members accumulate power and influence and acquire an important stake in the policy areas that are handled by the committee. The analyses in this chapter tells us that through their committee assignments, black state legislators tended to accumulate power and acquire influence in black interest policy areas more than in any other area. Consistent with the conclusion from chapter 2 regarding African American state representatives and legislative agenda-setting, the findings here indicate that the black legislators behaved like race representatives by attempting to insure that a black voice and perspective were heard at a very important stage of the legislative process.

In a recent study of committee assignment patterns in state legislatures, Kathlene Bratton and Kerry L. Haynie (n.d.) found that African American legislators were more likely than nonblack legislators to serve on education, health, and welfare committees, and that the bills they introduced were also more likely to be referred to one of those committees.[15] Serving on committees to which one's own proposals are referred provides substantial advantages in terms of advancing one's policy priorities through the legislative labyrinth. As Bratton and Haynie put it, "Racial and gender differences in committee service . . . facilitated black and female state legislators' ability to more effectively translate their policy agenda into policy outcomes" (n.d.:24). Based on two separate measures—saliency, measured as the percentage of all African American committee assignments devoted to a particular type of committee, and potential influence, calculated as the percentage of a committee's membership that is African American—we can conclude from the analyses above that African American legislators examined in this book were well positioned on standing committees to advance or protect a black interest agenda.

Interestingly, much like what has been chronicled among African American members of Congress (e.g., Canon 1995, 1999; Swain 1993), some of the data and analyses in this chapter indicate that, over time, there has been a broadening of the agendas and interests of African American legislators. Thus, once again, we have found evidence of African American representatives seeming to balance their concern for black interests with other interests that may be important to their districts, their legislative careers, or to both. So, in terms of their committee service, the African American legislators seemed to be both race representatives and "responsible legislators." That is, while they were well positioned on standing committees to advance a black interest agenda, they were also well positioned to exert influence on other important legislative matters as well.

CHAPTER 4

AFRICAN AMERICAN
POLITICAL INCORPORATION

A VIEW FROM THE STATES

After the passage of the 1965 Voting Rights Act, black politics was transformed from pressure or protest politics to the politics of electoral participation. This new politics served as an impetus for African Americans to compete for public office and led to significant gains in African American representation in government. A black presence in governmental institutions has important symbolic and psychological consequences for African Americans in particular, and all of American society in general. For example, Lani Guinier (1994) reports that an African American member of the 1989 Arkansas House of Representatives indicated that one reason that he worked to get other African Americans elected was to help undermine "the myth that some white kids might have that blacks can't serve or shouldn't be serving at the courthouse" (54). Like Virginia Sapiro's (1981) argument that increased descriptive representation of women in legislatures would dispel the perceptions and beliefs that politics is a "male domain," the increased presence of African Americans in public policy-making institutions challenges the notion that African Americans cannot or should not be trusted in positions of authority and power. The "new black politics," however, was not to be simply a struggle for inclusion. Inclusion was intended to be a means to substantive ends rather than merely a symbolic end unto itself. For example, one expectation has been that black inclusion would in some way challenge and change existing power structures and racial hierarchies as well as being a vehicle for transforming American political institutions.[1]

In recent years, it has become increasingly clear that descriptive representation or even simply articulating a race-based agenda may not be sufficient if African Americans are to have significant influence in public policy-making. Several scholars, most notably Browning, Marshall, and Tabb (1984), have persuasively argued that African American officeholders must achieve *political incorporation* as a precondition to having a meaningful effect on government policies and programs (see also Bobo and Gilliam 1990; Sonenshein 1993).

Political incorporation refers to the extent to which a group is represented in important and sometimes dominant coalitions in policy-making institutions. It is the degree "to which a group has been able to achieve a position from which strong and sustained influence can be exercised" (Browning, Marshall, and Tabb 1984:241). Browning and colleagues's measure of incorporation is a composite scale of the number or percentage of African American officeholders present in the policy-making arena, their presence in important leadership positions, and their active participation in dominant ruling coalitions.

High levels of incorporation are seen as necessary for a group to realize its political goals and objectives. Several studies have found political incorporation to be positively associated with increased governmental responsiveness to African American concerns and interests (Bobo and Gilliam 1990; Browning, Marshall, and Tabb 1984; Sonenshein 1993).

> A group that has achieved substantial political incorporation has taken a major step toward political equality. It is in a position to articulate its interests, its demands will be heard, and through the dominant coalition it can ensure that certain interests will be protected, even though it may not win on every issue. The group will have successfully opened the system and gained the kind of ability to make its interests prevail that other groups have already achieved.   (Browning, Marshall, and Tabb 1984:27)

Specifically, Browning and colleagues discovered that high levels of minority incorporation were accompanied by changes in urban policies such as the increased use of minority contractors, the appointment of more minorities to city commissions, the creation of police review boards, and improved city services in minority neighborhoods. Lawrence Bobo and Franklin D. Gilliam (1990) demonstrated that a link exists between African American incorporation and blacks' engagement and participation in the political process. They found that

African Americans living in high "black empowerment" areas were more knowledgeable of politics and more likely to vote and otherwise participate than those African Americans living in cities with low or no black empowerment.[2]

Are these apparent positive effects for African Americans from political incorporation limited to cities, or do black officeholders and black interests at other levels of government benefit from incorporation as well? To date, nearly all the research on minority-group political incorporation has been conducted at the municipal level. Therefore, our knowledge about the impact of this process outside of a city or urban context is somewhat limited.

LEGISLATURES AND POLITICAL INCORPORATION

Albert J. Nelson's 1991 book, *Emerging Influentials in State Legislatures: Women, Blacks, and Hispanics,* is one of the few studies to explore minority-group incorporation in a setting other than the city. He examined minority incorporation in forty-five lower state legislative chambers by constructing "influence indices" for women, African Americans, and Hispanics which were based on the party leadership positions and committee chairs that they held. In many respects, Nelson's findings for African Americans raised more questions about the process and significance of political incorporation in legislatures than he answered. Most of his results are statistically insignificant, counterintuitive, or contradictory to his hypotheses (Nelson 1991:114–16). A few examples of these findings follow.

> Black partial correlations also represent some unexpected results. Surprisingly, there is a significant but negative partial correlation . . . with education, a small but insignificant relationship with mental health and hospitals. These findings indicate educational expenditures are likely to be lower if black influence is greater. (114)

> Black influence in states with a unified Democratic government produces different results than reported above. . . . The results reported above indicate a positive, but insignificant, relationship between black influence and social service expenditures. That relationship is reversed here. I have found that there is marginally significant, but negative, correlations between black influence and social service expenditures. . . . If black influence increases from state to state, per capita expenditures for social services tend to decline. (116)

A somewhat restricted, overly narrow definition or construction of political incorporation might be part of the explanation for these findings. For example, Nelson constructed what he calls an index of "potential influence," which is based solely on leadership and committee chair positions and which takes into account whether legislators are in the majority or minority party (Nelson 1991:94). In this chapter, I seek to add to the knowledge about the nature and consequences of the concept of African American political incorporation by applying it in the five states used in this study. Building primarily on Browning, Marshall, and Tabb (1984), and to a lesser extent Nelson (1991), I have constructed an African American "political incorporation index" suited especially for legislatures. The incorporation index and the methods that I use here differ significantly from those employed by Nelson. The scale not only takes into account leadership positions and whether or not African Americans are in the majority party, it also accounts for the number of African Americans present in the legislature, the prestige or power committee assignments that they hold, and the tenure (i.e., seniority) of blacks in the legislature. Consequently, my conceptualization provides a somewhat more comprehensive representation of the potential that African Americans have to influence public policy. It recognizes that in order to achieve the capacity to exert strong and substantial influence in legislatures, African Americans not only need a continuous presence, but they also must obtain leadership positions and strategic committee assignments.

Specifically, my political incorporation scale for legislatures is a composite measure of six factors: (1) the number of African Americans in the legislature; (2) the percentage of the Democratic Party that African Americans constitute, (3) the number of prestige or power committee assignments they hold; (4) African American seniority levels; (5) leadership positions; and (6) the presence of an African American speaker, majority leader, or minority leader (table 4.1).[3] Descriptive representation is accounted for in this conceptualization of incorporation, but the scale relies most heavily on variables that are directly associated with power and influence in legislatures.[4] In other words, the African American political incorporation scale puts a premium on leadership positions, seniority, and strategic institutional positioning. Because of this, the expectation is that African American incorporation will be lower in the earlier legislative sessions when African American lawmakers were relatively new to state legislatures and less likely to have acquired key positions (i.e., 1969) than in the later sessions (i.e., 1989).[5]

African American political incorporation scores were computed for each of

TABLE 4.1

POLITICAL INCORPORATION INDEX FOR STATE LEGISLATURES

Variable	Value
Number of African Americans in legislature	Actual number
African American % of Democratic Party	Actual % (only if Democrats are majority)
Prestige committee assignments	1 point each assignment
Mean African American seniority in years	Actual average
Leadership positions*	2 points each position
Speaker, Majority/Minority Leader	3 points

*Prestige committees are the Appropriations, Budget, Finance/Taxation, Rules, and Ways and Means committees (see Smith and Deering 1980:87). Leadership positions include assistant majority/minority leader, party whips, assistant party whips, and committee chairs. The speaker, majority leader, and minority leader positions are counted separately.

the five state legislatures and the three legislative sessions examined in this book. First, one point was assigned for each African American in the legislature. Because it is clear that participation in a dominant coalition yields more substantive policy changes for minority groups than does descriptive representation alone (Browning, Marshall, and Tabb 1984; Nelson 1991; Sonenshein 1993), if the Democrats were the majority party I added points that equaled the percentage of the party that blacks constituted. This variable gives considerably more weight to those legislative sessions in which African Americans were part of a dominant or controlling coalition. For example, in New Jersey in 1979 the three African Americans in the Assembly made up 6 percent of the Democratic Party, and the Democrats were the majority party—thus six points more were added to the African American political incorporation score for New Jersey 1979. In 1989 six African Americans made up 15 percent of the Democratic Party; however, the Democrats were in the minority. Therefore, six points were added for the number of African Americans in the legislature, but no points for the percentage of the Democratic Party that they comprised were added to the political incorporation score for this session.

One point was added to the incorporation score for each assignment that a black legislator had on a prestige committee. Standing committee assignments are important in a legislature because most of a legislator's effect on public policy comes via his or her committee work. Prestige committees are a small group of powerful and highly coveted committees that deal with appropriations, taxation and budgeting issues, and the rules and procedures of the legislature. The conventional wisdom is that assignments on these committees tend to confer some extraordinary degree of power and influence to legislators (Francis 1989; Haynie n.d.; Smith and Deering 1990).

Seniority and holding formal leadership positions are important contributors to power and influence in legislatures. Senior representatives generally are more knowledgeable about legislative procedures, and this contributes to their being more effective in negotiating the legislative labyrinth (Meyer 1980; Weissert 1989). By virtue of the powers inherent in their positions, formal legislative leaders are decidedly more influential than rank-and-file legislators. The average seniority in years for black representatives was added to the African American political incorporation scores. Two points were assigned for each African American leader in a legislative session. Because of the extraordinary powers of the speaker and the majority and minority leaders (e.g., control over the legislative calendar and the committee assignment process), three points were added when an African American held one of these positions.

Because the analysis that follows is based on a limited sample of states, it is subject to all the caveats about generalizations. However, this analysis nevertheless provides some important insights into a virtually unexamined facet of African American legislative experience and behavior. The findings here can perhaps serve as the foundation for theory-building and more in-depth studies of this subject.

African American Political Incorporation in the Five States

In order to assess African American political incorporation in state legislatures, I assigned incorporation scores to the 1969, 1979, and 1989 legislative sessions of the lower house of the five state legislatures studied in this book (i.e., Arkansas, Illinois, Maryland, New Jersey, and North Carolina). African American political incorporation ranged from a low of 5 in North Carolina in 1969 to a high of 72 in Maryland's 1989 legislative session (see figure 4.1). Most importantly, the bar graphs in figure 4.1 show that, as expected, there was a dramatic growth in African American incorporation between 1969 and 1989. In all five states, African American incorporation was higher from one decade to the next. Considering all the states together, the average gain in incorporation between 1969 and

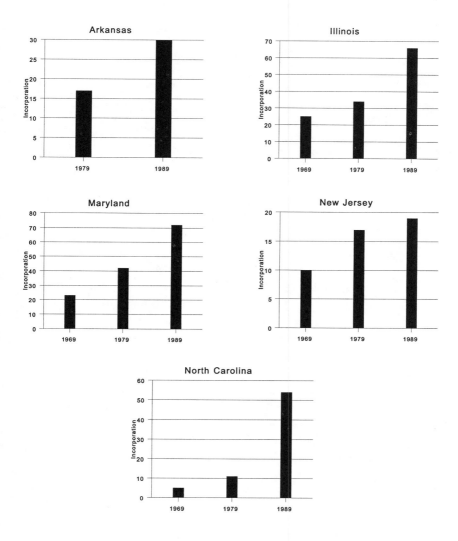

FIGURE 4.1 African American Political Incorporation in the Five States

TABLE 4.2

LEGISLATIVE SESSIONS GROUPED BY QUARTILES OF AFRICAN
AMERICAN POLITICAL INCORPORATION

Lowest			Highest
Arkansas 1969	Arkansas 1979	Illinois 1969	North Carolina 1989
North Carolina 1969	New Jersey 1979	Arkansas 1989	Illinois 1989
New Jersey 1969	New Jersey 1989	Illinois 1979	Maryland 1989
North Carolina 1979	Maryland 1969	Maryland 1979	

1989 was 283 percent. These data suggest that, again as expected, the status and clout of black state legislators has grown substantially over time.

Table 4.2 presents a ranking of the fifteen legislative sessions by quartiles of African American political incorporation.[6] Although African American incorporation and African American descriptive representation are highly correlated, $r = .92$ ($p \le .01$), the rankings in table 4.2 demonstrate the importance of other variables besides descriptive representation to the conceptualization and measurement of political incorporation. For example, although African Americans who served in Arkansas's 1989 legislative session made up a smaller percentage of their legislature than did African Americans in Maryland and Illinois in 1979 (see table 1.1), as a group the Arkansans achieved a higher level of political incorporation than did the blacks in both of these other legislative sessions. Similarly, in 1969, Illinois had a significantly higher percentage of African Americans in its legislature than Arkansas in 1989 (7.9 percent to 5.2 percent), but Arkansas 1989 placed higher in terms of African American incorporation. The number of prestige committee assignments held by African American legislators and their slightly higher level of seniority are responsible for these outcomes.

POLITICAL INCORPORATION AND
GOVERNMENTAL RESPONSIVENESS

The theory of political incorporation developed in studies like Browning, Marshall, and Tabb (1984) and Sonenshein (1993) maintains that increased African American incorporation in government results in significant and noticeable changes in public policy. Indeed, both of these studies found that changes in municipal politics and policies that were favorable to African Americans often followed periods of increased African American political incorporation on city councils. The question here is, has the growth in the power and status of African American state legislators translated into significant substantive results at the state level? That is, has there been any increased responsiveness to African American state legislators and to black policy interests that is related to the increases in African American incorporation in state legislatures?

Unlike previous studies, I treat responsiveness as having two closely related yet distinct dimensions—internal and external. *Internal responsiveness* refers to reactions to African American legislators inside the legislature, or to how black legislators themselves directly benefit from higher levels of political incorporation. The passage rates of bills introduced by African American legislators are used to measure and assess internal responsiveness in state legislatures. *External responsiveness,* on the other hand, refers to changes in public policy that are correlated to and explained, at least in part, by changes in African American representatives' level of incorporation. I address the question of whether political incorporation leads to external responsiveness by examining state expenditures in three policy areas: health, education, and social welfare. These policy categories include many of those issues that make up the core of black interests (see chapter 2; also see Bratton and Haynie 1999a; Canon 1999; Karnig and Welch 1980; Swain 1993).

The state expenditure data that I use for the analyses in this chapter are from three different time points: 1971–72, 1981–82, and 1991–1992. These years were selected to allow for some lag period between the beginning of a legislative term and the time when legislators who served in that session could reasonably be expected to have an impact on state spending. For example, the expenditure data that I use for the 1969 legislative sessions are the mean state expenditures for 1971–72, for 1979 they are the mean expenditures for 1981–82, and so on.

The argument regarding African American political incorporation is that it is a better predictor of institutional responsiveness than simple descriptive representation, and that the higher the level of incorporation, the more responsiveness there will be. Embedded in these expectations is the alternative explanation that African American descriptive representation by itself is sufficient to elicit favorable responses to black interests. That is to say, it is possible that institutions simply respond when there is an African American presence. Like the case for political incorporation, the more African Americans present in the legislatures, the more responsiveness we should expect. Thus while we are primarily interested in the effects of political incorporation on responsiveness, I also explore whether or not there is a relationship between descriptive representation (i.e., the percentage of legislators who are African American) and responsiveness, both internal and external.

INTERNAL RESPONSIVENESS

Because the incorporation scale developed and used here relies most heavily on variables that are associated with power and influence in legislatures, it is logical to expect political incorporation to be linked to internal institutional responsiveness. Individual legislators or groups of legislators like African Americans whose level of incorporation increases over time should benefit from this elevation in status and clout. Moreover, higher levels of incorporation should result in higher levels of responsiveness. The success that legislators have in getting the bills that they introduce passed is a useful and appropriate indicator of internal responsiveness. Bill passage in legislatures is often a *response* to the power, skill, and/or influence of the proposal's primary sponsors.

> Power is not identifiable until it is manifested in situations where one [legislator] gets his [or her] colleagues to do something they would otherwise not do. . . . The act of introducing a piece of legislation and requesting the [legislature] to act on it forces the members of the legislature to make decisions that would not otherwise be made. . . . In operational terms one congressman is more powerful than another when he [or she] is more effective in the passage of legislation."[7]

In other words, in making the decision to approve one bill as opposed to another, it is reasonable to argue that legislatures, in part, are being responsive to the status and stature of individual or small groups of representatives.[8]

Contrary to expectations, as measured by the percentage of their bill introductions that passed in the lower houses of the various state legislatures, African American lawmakers in general did not experience higher levels of internal responsiveness as their level of political incorporation increased (figure 4.2a). In fact, on average, a higher percentage of bills introduced by African American legislators passed in the legislative sessions with the lowest levels of African American incorporation. The passage rate in the quartile of legislative sessions with the lowest level of African American incorporation was 44.7 percent, compared to a passage rate of just 23.2 percent for the sessions with the highest amount of black incorporation. The pattern is the same when the legislative

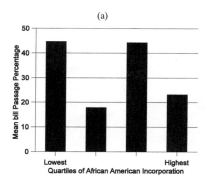
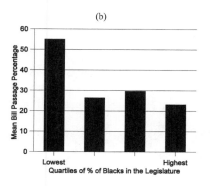

FIGURE 4.2 Political Incorporation, Descriptive Representation, and Mean Passage Rate of Bills Introduced by African American Legislators

sessions are grouped into quartiles of the percentage of African Americans in them (figure 4.2b). In this instance, not only did the quartile with the lowest levels of black descriptive representation have the highest level of responsiveness (55 percent passage rate), it is also the case that the sessions with the highest percentage of African American representatives were the least responsive (23.2 percent passage rate) to the rising power and status of black legislators.

The results in figure 4.2 suggest that neither African American political incorporation nor African American descriptive representation has a significant effect on the likelihood of passage of bills introduced by black legislators. The correlation data in table 4.3 support this finding. These findings are not expected.[9] According to these results, there is a negative and statistically insignificant

TABLE 4.3

CORRELATION OF *PASSAGE RATE OF BILLS INTRODUCED BY AFRICAN AMERICAN LEGISLATORS* WITH AFRICAN AMERICAN INCORPORATION AND AFRICAN AMERICAN DESCRIPTIVE REPRESENTATION $(N = 15)30$

	Average Percent of Bills Passed
Incorporation	−.08
Descriptive representation	−.16

correlation between the average passage rate of bills introduced by African American representatives and African American political incorporation. The results for the relationship between descriptive representation and bill passage rate was virtually the same—negative and not statistically significant. In other words, neither their increased presence nor their seemingly increased influence resulted in more internal institutional responsiveness for African American state legislators.

EXTERNAL RESPONSIVENESS

External responsiveness refers to changes in state public policy that are correlated to, and in part explained by, changes in African American representatives' level of political incorporation. State expenditures for health, education, and social welfare programs and services are what I use to measure this type of institutional responsiveness. My expectation, based on extant theories of political incorporation, is that African American political incorporation will be positively related to increased state spending in these policy areas.

HEALTH EXPENDITURES   The discrepancies in the quality of their health is perhaps the widest and most persistent gap between African Americans and whites. For example, there has been a long-standing racial divide in black-white life expectancy, infant mortality, and incidences of heart disease and cancer (Kochack, Maurer, and Rosenberg 1994; National Center for Health Statistics 1994). These gaps are large and are growing.

> In 1995 the life expectancy for blacks was about 10 percent shorter than that for whites (seventy years for blacks, compared to seventy-seven for whites), the infant mortality rate was double for blacks (15.1 deaths per 100,000 births for blacks, compared to 7.6). . . . The death rate for women with breast cancer fell by 10 percent for all women between 1990 and 1996, but did not change for blacks (and now stands at 27.5 deaths per 100,00 for blacks, compared to 21 for all women). . . . The cancer rate among black men has risen by 67 percent since the early 1960s, but only about 11 percent among white men. Death caused by stroke and heart disease are also substantially more frequent among blacks, though the gap between blacks and whites did not increase between 1990 and 1995.   (Canon 1999:24–25)

Addressing these conditions is a perennial concern of the black community.

Figure 4.3 provides information on the relationship between African American political incorporation, African American descriptive representation, and

(a)

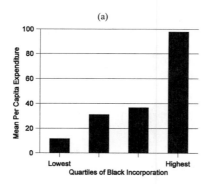

(b)

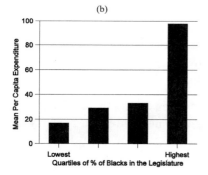

(c)

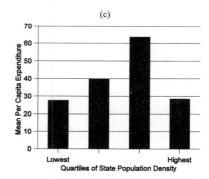

FIGURE 4.3 Political Incorporation, Descriptive Representation, Population Density, and State *Health Expenditures*

state health expenditures. The findings comport perfectly with the arguments of both the political incorporation and descriptive representation perspectives. The three legislative sessions with the highest levels of African American incorporation (figure 4.3a) spent significantly more per person on health programs than the four legislative sessions with the lowest levels of incorporation ($98 to $12).[10] Likewise, the three legislative sessions with the greatest proportion of African Americans in them (figure 4.3b) spent significantly more than the four sessions with the least ($98 to $17).

The correlation results in table 4.4 confirm the findings in figure 4.3. Both political incorporation and descriptive representation are significantly corre-

TABLE 4.4

CORRELATION OF PER CAPITA STATE SPENDING FOR *HEALTH* WITH
AFRICAN AMERICAN INCORPORATION AND AFRICAN AMERICAN
DESCRIPTIVE REPRESENTATION
$(N = 15)$

	Health Expenditures
Incorporation	.84*
Descriptive representation	.74*

Note: Descriptive representation is measured as the percentage of African Americans in the legislature.
*$p < .001$

lated to state health spending. Of these two, African American political incorporation is more closely related to responsiveness.

EDUCATION EXPENDITURES   Better educational achievement is widely considered the most effective means for improving the health, social, and economic conditions of the African American community. In fact, previous research and analyses (as presented in chapter 2) demonstrate that African American legislators at the state level are more likely than other state representatives to introduce legislation supportive of education (Bratton and Haynie 1999a). Thus spending by states to improve or provide more educational opportunities is an outcome that is desired by African American legislators and African American citizens alike.[11]

The arguments that institutions respond only when African Americans are present in the legislature, and the greater the black presence, the more responsiveness there is likely to be, seems to be strongly supported by the results in figure 4.4b. Indeed, when the state legislative sessions are grouped into quartiles according to the percentage of African Americans in them, those with higher proportions of black legislators spend more on education than those with lower proportions.

As for political incorporation, a cursory look at the relationship between African American incorporation and per capita education expenditures that is represented in figure 4.4a provides little empirical support for the hypothesis that higher levels of incorporation will lead to more spending for education initiatives. However, results from the correlation analyses reported in table 4.5 suggest a different conclusion. These data show that, in fact, African American

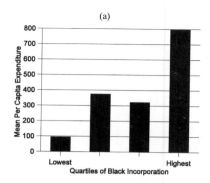

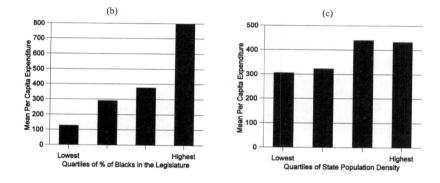

FIGURE 4.4 Political Incorporation, Descriptive Representation, Population Density, and State *Education Expenditures*

political incorporation is more closely connected to spending for education than is the percentage of African Americans in the legislature. These data also confirm the figure 4.4b findings of a relationship between African American descriptive representation and state responsiveness in this policy area.

SOCIAL WELFARE EXPENDITURES   High unemployment and large numbers of people living below the poverty level have long been a part of the African American experience. In every year between 1970 and 1990, nearly one-third of African Americans lived in poverty. Moreover, the African American unemployment rate was consistently at least twice that of whites during this same twenty-year span (U.S. Department of Commerce 1992). Consequently, African Ameri-

TABLE 4.5

CORRELATION OF PER CAPITA STATE SPENDING FOR *EDUCATION*
WITH AFRICAN AMERICAN INCORPORATION AND AFRICAN
AMERICAN DESCRIPTIVE REPRESENTATION ($N = 15$)

	Education Expenditures
Incorporation	.59[*]
Descriptive representation	.51[*]

Note: Descriptive representation is measured as the percentage of African Americans in the legislature.

[*]$p < .05$

cans tend to strongly favor increased support and spending for social welfare and economic redistribution programs. Redistribution programs are those government policies and/or services that reallocate societal resources. They transfer economic resources from those who have the most and who have gained the most from economic development to those who have been left behind or who are less well-off, like the elderly, the disabled, the poor, the unemployed, the sick, and children. All the policy areas discussed and analyzed in this chapter fall within the redistribution category (see, for example, Peterson 1995:16). The 1984–1988 National Black Election Panel Study contains survey results that attest to African Americans' support for these types of policies. For instance, the study found that 82 and 79 percent of African Americans favored increased government spending for job creation and Medicare, respectively. Thus, greater state spending for social welfare programs is another reasonable indicator of responsiveness toward black interests.

The graphs in figure 4.5 offer support for both the political incorporation and the descriptive representation hypotheses. As the level of incorporation increases, so does per capita state expenditures for social welfare (figure 4.5a). The three legislative sessions with the highest level of African American political incorporation spent on average $467 per person for social welfare programs, compared to only $59 per person spent by the sessions with the lowest level. Similarly, larger amounts of money are spent on social welfare when the proportion of African Americans in the legislature is higher (figure 4.5b). Those sessions with the greatest proportion of African Americans average $467 in per capita expenditures, and those with the lowest proportion average $89 per person.

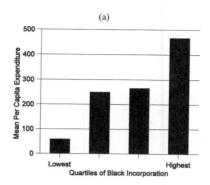

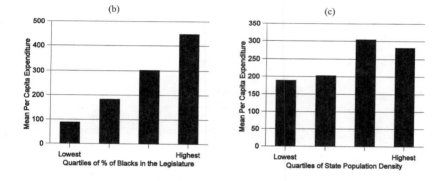

FIGURE 4.5 Political Incorporation, Descriptive Representation, Population Density, and State *Welfare Expenditures*

The correlations in table 4.6 indicate that black incorporation is slightly more closely related to responsiveness in welfare spending than simple descriptive representation. However, it is clear that both African American incorporation and black descriptive representation are potentially key factors in influencing expenditures in this area. More sophisticated testing of both possibilities is presented later in this chapter.

AN AGGREGATE MEASURE OF POLICY RESPONSIVENESS

In an attempt to clarify further the relationship of African American political incorporation to responsiveness, I combined state expenditures for health, ed-

TABLE 4.6

CORRELATION OF PER CAPITA STATE SPENDING FOR *WELFARE* WITH
AFRICAN AMERICAN INCORPORATION AND AFRICAN AMERICAN
DESCRIPTIVE REPRESENTATION $(N = 15)$

	Welfare Expenditures
Incorporation	.63*
Descriptive representation	.60*

Note: Descriptive representation is measured as the percentage of African Americans in the legislature.
*p < .01

TABLE 4.7

CORRELATION OF TOTAL PER CAPITA STATE SPENDING FOR
REDISTRIBUTION PROGRAMS WITH AFRICAN AMERICAN
INCORPORATION AND AFRICAN AMERICAN DESCRIPTIVE
REPRESENTATION $(N = 15)$

	Redistributive Expenditures
Incorporation	.61**
Descriptive representation	.55*

Note: Total per capita redistributive expenditures is the sum of per capita state spending for health, education, and welfare programs. Descriptive representation is measured as the percentage of African Americans in the legislature.
**p < .01
*p < .05

ucation, and welfare into an aggregate measure of total state per capita redistribution spending. This combined measure allows for the assessment of a state's overall responsiveness to black incorporation. The correlation data presented in table 4.7 indicates that African American incorporation is more closely related to overall policy responsiveness relative to black interests than descriptive representation.

The findings reported in figure 4.6 mirror the patterns that resulted when the spending categories were analyzed separately, and they are generally consistent with both the political incorporation and descriptive representation hypotheses. As measured by total state redistribution expenditures, the legislative

(a)

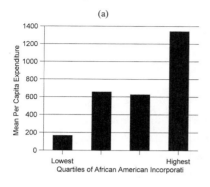

(b)

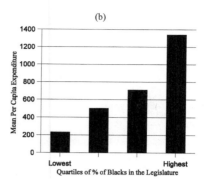

FIGURE 4.6 Political Incorporation, Descriptive Representation, and Total State *Redistributive Expenditures*

sessions in which African American representatives attained the greatest levels of incorporation generated more responsiveness to black interests than did the other sessions. There was a $1,176.00 difference in expenditures between the quartile with the highest levels of black incorporation and the quartile with the lowest (figure 4.6a). Likewise, legislative sessions with more descriptive representation of African Americans generated more expenditures for black interest programs than did sessions with smaller proportions of African Americans in them (figure 4.6b).The difference in redistributive spending between the highest and lowest quartiles in this instance was $1,109.00.

Discussion

Whether there is a noticeable and significant relationship between African American political incorporation and institutional or governmental responsiveness to black interests, and whether or not incorporation provides a better explanation of such responsiveness than does descriptive representation, were the questions that began this section. The findings above indicate that greater black incorporation does not necessarily translate into more internal responsiveness for black legislators. I find a negative and statistically insignificant correlation between African American political incorporation and the passage rate of bills introduced by black lawmakers. The results for the relationship between descriptive representation and bill passage rate was virtually the same— negative and not statistically significant.

With regard to external responsiveness, however, the analyses thus far show that African American incorporation is indeed associated with important changes in state policy. African American incorporation has been found to be positively linked with state expenditures for health, education, and social welfare programs. The higher the level of incorporation, the more responsiveness there is. That is, legislative sessions with higher African American incorporation spend more on these redistribution programs than sessions with lower black incorporation. Descriptive representation, measured as the percentage of legislators who are African American, is also shown to be linked to external responsiveness to black interests. However, incorporation appears to be the more closely related variable of the two. Incorporation is more highly correlated to state spending in each of the separate policy areas, as well as to total state redistributive spending.

All of these analyses and results are quite suggestive, yet they are neither conclusive evidence that African American political incorporation has a significant effect on state redistributive spending, nor are they proof that incorporation provides a more empirically satisfying explanation of state responsiveness than descriptive representation. Only after controlling for other factors that potentially influence state expenditure decisions will it be possible to identify the precise effects of political incorporation and descriptive representation. I now turn to multivariate regression analyses with which such controls are possible.

POLITICAL INCORPORATION, DESCRIPTIVE REPRESENTATION, AND BLACK INTERESTS: A MULTIVARIATE ANALYSIS

To determine the distinctive influence that both African American political incorporation and African American descriptive representation have on governmental responsiveness to black interests, I estimated multivariate regression models using the ordinary least squares (OLS) procedure.[12] As with the correlation analyses above, state per capita expenditures for health, education, and social welfare, and the total per capita expenditures for redistribution programs are the dependent variables. Along with incorporation and descriptive representation, the states' poverty rate, percentage of people living in urban areas, and tax capacity are included as possible explanatory variables.[13] A state's poverty rate could significantly influence its redistributive expenditures. States with relatively high percentages of poor people might view the alleviation of poverty as a priority, or they may face political pressure to address the needs of the poor from various interest groups and thus be inclined to spend more for redistribution programs. Because their populations are often poorer, less educated, and more likely to be unemployed, the social welfare needs of cities might be greater than those of rural and suburban communities. The higher the percentage of a state's population living in urban areas, the more that state is likely to spend for social welfare programs. Tax capacity is a measure of the amount of revenue a state can raise at a given tax rate (Advisory Commission on Intergovernmental Relations 1982). State spending is expected to be higher in those states with more fiscal resources. Therefore, it is important to include tax capacity as a control.

Because African American political incorporation, as conceptualized here, includes a measure for the number of blacks in the legislature, there is high multicollinearity between the variables African American incorporation and African American descriptive representation. Therefore, models that include both variables simultaneously are problematic. When high multicollinearity exists, the parameter estimates of a model become unreliable and one runs the risk of accepting the null hypothesis that there is no relationship between a dependent and independent variable when the two are in actuality linked. Consequently, in the analyses that follow, I estimate two separate regression models for each expenditure category. One model includes political incorporation, the state's poverty rate, the percentage of the state's population living in urban areas, and the state's tax capacity as the control variables. The second model includes all of these same variables except political incorporation is replaced by descriptive representation, which is measured as the percentage of legislators who are African American.

RESULTS

Recall that the argument regarding African American political incorporation is that, because the measure of the concept encompasses the variables that are directly associated with power and influence in legislatures, it is a better predictor of responsiveness than simple descriptive representation. OLS regression results for a state's health expenditures are reported in table 4.8. Estimates of bivariate models with political incorporation and descriptive representation as explanatory variables are presented in columns one and two, respectively (Models I and II). The coefficients are positive and statistically significant for

TABLE 4.8

THE EFFECTS OF AFRICAN AMERICAN POLITICAL INCORPORATION AND
AFRICAN AMERICAN DESCRIPTIVE REPRESENTATION ON STATE PER
CAPITA *HEALTH EXPENDITURES* $(N = 15)$

Independent Variables	Model I	Model II	Model III	Model IV
Incorporation	1.42***	—	1.86***	—
	(.249)		(0.28)	
Descriptive representation	—	6.21***	—	10.04***
		(1.56)		(1.95)
Poverty rate	—	—	4.12**	6.04**
			(1.85)	(2.39)
Population density	—	—	.06*	.04
			(0.03)	(0.03)
Tax capacity	—	—	−.29	−.25
			(0.69)	(0.83)
Intercept	.575	.193	−58.34	−96.47
	(8.79)	(12.6)	(76.4)	(91.3)
R²	.71	.55	.83	.76

Note: Standard errors are in parentheses. See Appendix 2 for a description of the variables and a list of data sources.
***$p \leq .01$
**$p \leq .05$
*$p \leq .10$

both political incorporation and descriptive representation, which tells us that both variables have an effect on state spending for health programs. However, as indicated by the R-square values, the incorporation model (Model I) explains more of the variance in health expenditures than does incorporation.

In Models III and IV of table 4.8, state poverty rates, population densities, and tax capacities are included with political incorporation and descriptive representation as possible explanatory variables. The results are similar to those from the bivariate models in that both incorporation and descriptive representation are in the expected direction, and both are statistically significant at the $p \leq .01$ level. For each unit increase in African American incorporation, the states spent an additional $1.86 per person for health services. For every percentage increase in African American descriptive representation, state health expenditures rose slightly more than ten dollars per state resident. Both models also indicate that the level of poverty in states contributes to how much states spend for health programs.

Although a comparison of the R-square values shows that the incorporation model provides a slightly better explanation of state spending for health, both of the R-squares are relatively high and therefore each of the models is satisfactory and acceptable on its own terms. In other words, as measured by state expenditures for health programs and services, these data offer support for the hypothesis that responsiveness to black interests increases as African American representatives become more incorporated into the power structures of legislative institutions; and these data also support the proposition that African American descriptive representation by itself is sufficient to elicit favorable responses to black interests. Thus, similar to the findings in the previous two chapters, here it appears that simple descriptive representation alone provides some important tangible or substantive results vis-à-vis black interests.

The regression results for the effects of incorporation and descriptive representation on state expenditures for education are presented in table 4.9. Here,

TABLE 4.9

THE EFFECTS OF AFRICAN AMERICAN POLITICAL INCORPORATION AND
AFRICAN AMERICAN DESCRIPTIVE REPRESENTATION ON STATE PER
CAPITA *EDUCATION EXPENDITURES* ($N = 15$)

Independent Variables	Model I	Model II	Model III	Model IV
Incorporation	10.14*	—	15.51**	—
	(3.82)		(4.58)	
Descriptive representation	—	44.1*	—	85.99**
		(20.2)		(26.8)
Poverty rate	—	—	65.06*	82.51*
			(29.5)	(33.1)
Population density	—	—	.06	.65
			(0.41)	(0.03)
Tax capacity	—	—	2.78	2.76
			(11.0)	(11.4)
Intercept	76.49	75.82	−1462.2	−1789.7
	(134.8)	(157.6)	(1219)	(1260)
R^2	.35	.27	.58	.55

Note: Standard errors are in parentheses. See Appendix 2 for a description of the variables and a list of data sources.
**$p \leq .01$
*$p \leq .05$

as with the models for health expenditures, both African American incorporation and African American descriptive representation have a significant and positive effect on governmental responsiveness. The parameter estimate for political incorporation in Model III indicates that states spend, on average, $15.50 per person more on education with every unit increase of African American political incorporation. For every percentage increase in the proportion of the legislature that African Americans comprise, average per capita expenditures for education increases by $86 (Model IV). It is interesting to note that here, just as with health expenditures (table 4.8), a state's poverty rate, as expected, has a significant effect on how much a state spends for education. The magnitude of the parameter estimates for poverty show that it has a powerful influence on this category of state spending.

In both the bivariate and multivariate regressions, the incorporation models (I and III), fit the data better than the descriptive representation models (II and IV), but only slightly so in the case of the multivariate analyses. It appears, then, that neither model is especially superior to the other. This suggests that the substantive explanations embedded in the theory of political incorporation do not take us much further in understanding responsiveness to black interests than arguments that suggest that simply having African Americans present in policy-making institutions leads to attention and action on blacks' policy concerns.

The regression results for social welfare expenditures presented in table 4.10 follow the pattern found in the previous two sets of analyses. In the bivariate models, for example, the coefficients are positive and statistically significant for both political incorporation and descriptive representation, which tells us that each of the variables has an effect on state expenditures for social welfare programs. The incorporation model (Model I) explains slightly more of the variance in state welfare spending ($R^2 = .40$) than Model II, the descriptive representation model ($R^2 = .37$).

Regarding the multivariate models (Models III and IV), the pattern is again similar to what we found with the bivariate models, in that both the incorporation and descriptive representation variables are in the expected direction and are statistically significant at the $p \leq .01$ level. Each one-unit increase in African American incorporation results in an average increase of $7.87 per person in state spending for welfare programs (Model III). For every 1 percent increase in the proportion of the legislature that African Americans comprise, average expenditures for education increases by $44.44 per person (Model IV). Each of the models also indicates that the level of poverty in states contributes to how

TABLE 4.10

THE EFFECTS OF AFRICAN AMERICAN POLITICAL INCORPORATION AND
AFRICAN AMERICAN DESCRIPTIVE REPRESENTATION ON STATE PER
CAPITA *SOCIAL WELFARE EXPENDITURES* ($N = 15$)

Independent Variables	Model I	Model II	Model III	Model IV
Incorporation	5.95***	—	7.87***	—
	(2.03)		(2.34)	
Descriptive representation	—	28.5***	—	44.44***
		(10.4)		(13.4)
Poverty rate	—	—	33.94**	43.34**
			(15.1)	(16.5)
Population density	—	—	.33	.30
			(0.21)	(0.21)
Tax capacity	—	—	5.77	5.63
			(5.63)	(5.69)
Intercept	69.03	51.32	−1107.1*	−1276.7
	(71.4)	(80.4)	(621.9)	(629.3)
R²	.40	.37	.64	.63

Note: Standard errors are in parentheses. See Appendix 2 for a description of the variables and a list of data sources.
***$p \le .01$
**$p \le .05$
*$p \le .10$

much states spend for social welfare programs. For example, with the incorporation model, for every 1 percent increase in a state's poverty rate, about $34 more per person are spent in the social welfare policy area. With the descriptive representation model, the figure is a little more than $43 more per person. That the R-squares of the multivariate regression models in table 4.10 are almost identical (.64 *versus* .63) is evidence that supports both the hypothesis that responsiveness to black interests increases as African American representatives' level of political incorporation increases, and the proposition that the mere presence of African Americans in state legislatures has positive consequences for black interests.

The dependent variable in the final set of regressions is the total state per capita expenditures for redistribution programs. Total redistributive expenditures are the combined state expenditures for health, education, and social wel-

TABLE 4.11

THE EFFECTS OF AFRICAN AMERICAN POLITICAL INCORPORATION AND
AFRICAN AMERICAN DESCRIPTIVE REPRESENTATION ON TOTAL STATE
REDISTRIBUTIVE EXPENDITURES ($N = 15$)

Independent Variables	Model I	Model II	Model III	Model IV
Incorporation	17.37**	—	25.42**	—
	(6.29)		(7.45)	
Descriptive representation	—	78.66**	—	142.25**
		(32.9)		(43.2)
Poverty rate	—	—	108.58*	138.08*
			(47.9)	(16.5)
Population density	—	—	1.17	1.07
			(0.62)	(0.67)
Tax capacity	—	—	9.20	8.97
			(17.9)	(18.35)
Intercept	162.4	140.7	−2804.7	−3346.9
	(221.83)		(1981.7)	(2027.2)
R^2	.37	.30	.60	.59

Note: Standard errors are in parentheses. See Appendix 2 for a description of the
variables and a list of data sources.
**$p \leq .01$
*$p \leq .05$

fare. This aggregate measure allows for the assessment of a state's overall responsiveness to black interests. Table 4.11 shows the results of regressions run
for the total per capita state redistributive spending category. The findings generally confirm the interpretations derived from the analyses in tables 4.7 to 4.9.
The political incorporation and the descriptive representation variables are
positive and statistically significant in all the models. Moreover, there is virtually no difference in the explanatory power of the two multivariate models. The
incorporation model (Model III) explains 60 percent of the variance in per
capita state redistributive spending, and the descriptive representation models
explains 59 percent. Thus, as was the case with the individual regression analyses conducted for health, education, and social welfare expenditures, these data
for total per capita redistributive spending offer evidence to support the hypothesis that responsiveness to black interests increases as African American
representatives become more incorporated into the power structures of legisla-

tive institutions; and these data also support the proposition that African American descriptive representation by itself is sufficient to elicit favorable responses to black interests.

CONCLUSION

Political incorporation refers to the extent to which a group is strategically positioned to exercise significant influence over the policy-making process within political institutions. Increasing their level or degree of political incorporation is widely viewed as an important and perhaps necessary goal for cohesive political subgroups who are numerical minorities in political institutions. This is considered to be especially true for groups that have previously been excluded, legally and otherwise, from the governmental process. African American state legislators are one such group. The argument is that higher levels of political incorporation puts such groups in a more advantageous position to insure that their personal interests as well as the interests of their constituents are heard and seriously considered during debates over policy choices.

> A group that is intensely concerned about governmental policies, but has not gained access to the policy-making process has not achieved significant political equality. A group that achieves substantial incorporation—beyond the right to vote and simple representation—is in a strong position to change government policy in areas of special concern to them. Substantial incorporation, including partnership in a dominant coalition, provides an especially strong form of access to policy making, bringing with it opportunities to affect every stage of the policy process.
>
> (Browning, Marshall, and Tabb 1984:243)

Conceptualized here as a composite measure of the number of African Americans in the legislature, the percentage of the Democratic Party that African Americans constitute, the number of prestige standing committee assignments and leadership positions that blacks hold, African American seniority, and the presence of an African American speaker, majority leader, or minority leader, the analyses above show that African American state legislators' degrees of political incorporation and, consequently, their status and clout, have grown significantly since 1970. In the five state legislatures studied in this book, the average increase in African American incorporation between 1969 and 1989 was 283 percent. Like the previous research on minority group incorporation in urban or municipal politics (e.g., Browning, Marshall, and Tabb 1984; Sonenshein 1993), I found this growth in African American incorporation in state legislatures to be positively linked to what I call external institutional responsiveness to black interests. In general, the higher the level of black incorporation, the more states spent on health, education, and social welfare programs.

Notwithstanding the significant correlations between African American incorporation and state spending in the black interest policy areas, the regression analyses in this chapter also yielded the somewhat surprising finding that the effects of higher African American incorporation are not decidedly superior to the effects of increased black descriptive representation. Not only is this finding counterintuitive, to some extent, it is also contrary to the arguments and conclusions of the most comprehensive study of minority-group political incorporation to date—Browning, Marshall, and Tabb's *Protest Is Not Enough* (1984). While acknowledging the importance of descriptive representation to the governmental process, Browning and colleagues conclude that "in our ten cities political incorporation of blacks and Hispanics led to increased policy responsiveness to minorities. This political variable best predicts the policy responsiveness, and is a better predictor of policy responsiveness than minority population" (250–51). Here, while it is indeed the case that black political incorporation had positive and significant effects on spending in each of the black interest policy areas, and that the multivariate incorporation regression models explained slightly more of the variance in these expenditures, it appears that it is also true that the mere presence of African Americans in state legislatures, regardless of their political incorporation status, was sufficient to yield significant institutional and governmental responsiveness relative to black interests. Thus African American representatives, and consequently African American citizens, seem to benefit almost as much from the simple presence of blacks in state legislatures as they do from high levels of African American incorporation in these same institutions.

The differences in the findings here and in those of Browning and colleagues may be due to the small and somewhat limited sample of states and years used in this study. However, Nelson's (1991) study of minority-group influence in state legislatures, which utilizes a forty-five state sample, reaches conclusions about African American incorporation not unlike the ones here.[14] Alternatively, the differences might mean that political incorporation has different degrees of importance and varying consequences or benefits for African Americans, depending on the particular political context in question. That is to say, in comparison to descriptive representation, political incorporation may be more meaningful and may yield more tangible benefits in local political settings, such as city councils and county commissions, than in state legislatures where there are multiple centers of power and power itself is generally more diffuse. It could also be the case that the effects of African American incorporation are less detectable in larger institutional settings.

Finally, we should note that although the incorporation and descriptive representation models were similar in their predictive and explanatory powers, from a practical point of view it is probable that future increases in African American influence in legislatures will come more from increased political incorporation than from increases in the number of African Americans elected to these bodies. For example, given both the current political and legal climate regarding the creation of majority-minority legislative districts, and the fact that, even under the best of circumstances, there is a finite number of such districts that can be drawn (e.g., Swain 1993), it is likely that, in any given state legislature, the number of African American legislators acquiring more seniority, leadership positions, and prestige committee assignments will increase at a faster rate than the number of new African Americans elected to them. Consequently, greater incorporation may be the most efficient and effective short-term strategy for assuring the substantive representation of black interests in state legislatures. However, an increased reliance on political incorporation may present African American representatives with a profound dilemma. One cost of achieving higher levels of incorporation might be that African American legislators will be required to behave less like race men and women and display a more overt commitment to the values of the larger legislative institution. For example, in order to increase their power and influence, black legislators might be pressured to seek more assignments on prestige committees and fewer on the committees whose jurisdictions include traditional black interest areas. If such trade-offs become necessary, greater incorporation of African American legislators may be inconsistent with efforts to articulate and promote the interests of African American constituents, who, as a group, remain economically and politically deprived, and African American legislators will be required to engage in a delicate, precarious, and perhaps impossible balancing act.

CHAPTER 5

RACE AND PEER EVALUATIONS OF AFRICAN AMERICAN LEGISLATORS

A CASE STUDY*

How open, receptive, and responsive state legislatures are to African American representation is one of the primary questions considered in this book. African American political incorporation, the subject of chapter 4, is one measure of institutional openness or responsiveness. Another equally important, albeit less tangible, measure of openness is how African American legislators are viewed by their colleagues. Previous studies have demonstrated that, because of their race, African American candidates for public office are often perceived and evaluated less favorably by voters (Baker and Kleppner 1986; Carsey 1995; Citrin, Green, and Sears 1990; Giles and Buckner 1993; Glaser 1994; Kinder 1986; Kinder and Sears 1981; Sigelman et al. 1995; Terkildsen, 1993). Some of this research has concluded that the perception of racial threat is instrumental in provoking negative reactions to African American candidates from whites (Giles and Buckner 1993; Glaser 1994; Key 1949; Pettigrew 1976; Wolfinger 1974). Does this dynamic continue once African Americans are elected and take their places in governmental institutions? That is, how are African American legislators viewed by their peers? Do they elicit a racially based negative reaction from within the legislature similar to what they might face out-

---

*The data and analyses used in this chapter are drawn from Haynie (1999).

side of it? This chapter addresses these questions by examining the role that race plays in other legislators' perceptions and evaluations of African American legislators in the North Carolina General Assembly.

The answer to these questions potentially has significant theoretical and practical political implications. For example, if African American representatives as a group are routinely perceived negatively, this could be an indication that they and any unique or distinctive interests that they represent may not be well received in an important and increasingly relevant policy-making institution. We know, for example, that African American legislators are the primary advocates of so-called black interest legislation (chapter 2; also see Bratton and Haynie 1992, 1999a; Haynie 1994; Hedge, Button, and Spear 1996; Miller 1990). Thus, if African American representatives are viewed unfavorably by their peers, it is possible that black interests will receive inadequate articulation and deliberation by policy-making institutions as a whole. Also, being perceived negatively could result in African American legislators' being unable to forge coalitions in support of their overall policy agendas. Moreover, such a finding would call into question any expectations, claims, or insinuations that American political institutions are inherently color-blind or race neutral.

LEGISLATIVE EFFECTIVENESS

Because, by their very nature, they involve subjective evaluations, studies of legislative effectiveness provide us with the data and means to assess whether legislators' race matters significantly with regard to how they are perceived. In the scholarly literature focusing on legislative effectiveness, variations in effectiveness have been measured and explained using individual attributes,[1] institutional positions, and behavioral indicators (e.g., Eulau 1962; Frantzich 1979; Hamm, Harmel, and Thompson 1983; Jewell 1969; Meyer 1980; Olson and Nonidez 1972; Weissert 1989).[2] For example, Katherine Meyer (1980) developed two causal models of legislative effectiveness using twelve explanatory variables. Her analyses found that education, prior political experience, seniority, and holding formal leadership positions were significantly related to a legislator's having a reputation for being effective. To this list, Carol Weissert (1989) adds the variable of whether or not a legislator is an attorney. The findings of a study by David M. Olson and Cynthia T. Nonidez (1972) suggest that it is through legislative activities like committee work and largely nonlegislative activities like casework that members of the U.S. House of Representatives gain reputations for being effective. Stephen Frantzich (1979) equates legislative effectiveness with legislative success. Using three behavioral indicators of effectiveness—the number of bills that each legislator had passed by the House, the number enacted into law, and the percentage of their bill introductions that passed in the House—Frantzich found party affiliation, formal leadership positions, seniority, and electoral security to be important explanatory variables.

Surprisingly, this is one of the first studies to include the race of the representative as a variable with potentially significant consequences for perceptions of effectiveness. The omission of race as a possible factor in the previous literature is particularly noteworthy given that race is one of the most salient attributes in American politics, and given our knowledge of the role that racial considerations play in the evaluations of African American candidates.

Notwithstanding the variety of meanings and measures of legislative effectiveness found in the previous literature, my goal here is not to determine or assess whether African Americans are "in fact" more or less effective than other representatives. Instead, the primary concern of this chapter is to explore what, if any, effect race has on how black legislators are viewed by their peers. I am interested in evaluations of legislative effectiveness only as indicators or surrogate measures of perceptions.

What effect should we expect the race of black legislators to have on perceptions of their legislative effectiveness? Studies of American race relations and the theoretical literature on racial attitudes and elections offer three possible answers to this question. One potential answer is that (everything else being equal) African American legislators will be perceived as less effective than other representatives. This expectation is rooted in the long history of racism and discrimination against blacks in the United States, and is a logical extension of the conclusions reached in several studies of voter attitudes. For example, as previously mentioned, many studies have shown that African American candidates are often evaluated less favorably than nonblack candidates by white voters because of their race (Baker and Kleppner 1986; Kinder and Sears 1981; Pettigrew 1976; Sears, Citrin, and Kosterman 1987; Sigelman et al. 1995; Terkildsen 1993).[3]

A second possible answer is that the race of black legislators will have no effect on perceptions of their legislative effectiveness. This expectation is reasonable given the reported decline in racist and nondiscriminatory attitudes among whites (Schuman, Steeh, and Bobo 1985; Smith 1995). In this post-civil rights era, nonblacks may now be more inclined to view African Americans as equals.

The third answer suggested by the scholarly literature is that the effects of race are conditional. That is, African American legislators will be evaluated positively when they possess desirable attributes such as leadership positions and seniority. As I previously mentioned, earlier research (e.g., Meyer 1980; Weissert 1989) found such characteristics to be positively correlated with perceived legislative effectiveness. This expectation is consistent with the "extremity effects" concept discussed by Carol Sigelman et al. (1995). The extremity effects concept suggests that there is a tendency for people to form "especially positive impressions of competent or attractive outgroup members and especially negative impressions of incompetent or unattractive outgroup members" (247). Seniority, leadership positions, and prestige committee assignments are among the desirable or attractive attributes for legislators. Thus it is reasonable to expect that when African American lawmakers possess such qualities, their colleagues will tend to have positive impressions of them.

In sum, the previous literature suggests three possible effects of race on the evaluation of African American officeholders: the impact is significant and negative; it is nonexistent; or the impact of race is conditional. I examine the applicability of these three alternatives below.

DATA AND METHODS

In my examination of how black legislators are viewed by other legislators, I use data from only one of the five legislatures—the North Carolina General Assembly. Ideally, this analysis would include data from the other four legislatures discussed in this book, and it would be comparative in approach in order for the findings to be somewhat generalizable. However, as is often the case with state-level studies, cross-state comparisons are not possible because comparable data do not exist. Although some type of effectiveness ratings takes place in some of the other states, the criteria, methods, and dependent variables used to assess "effectiveness" vary significantly from state to state. For example, in Arkansas the effectiveness assessments are conducted solely by capitol newspaper reporters, and legislators are judged based on their intelligence and the degree to which they have an open mind. The criteria used for some states evaluates effectiveness in terms of a members' integrity, fairness, and willingness to put the public interest ahead of partisanship and personal ambition. In still others, effectiveness, energy, flexibility, and potential are among a list of independent variables used to rank legislators from "best to worst."[4] Because of these vast differences in criteria and methods, the ideal of cross-state comparisons is not feasible.

Data on legislative effectiveness collected by the North Carolina Center for Public Policy Research (NCCPPR) will be used to address the question of what role race plays in the evaluation of African American legislators. After each legislative session since 1977, the North Carolina Center for Public Policy Research has conducted a survey to assess how effective state senators and representatives are considered to be. Lobbyists who are registered with the legislature, members of the press corps who regularly cover legislative events, and all legislators are asked to rate, on a scale from one to ten, every member of the General Assembly in terms of their effectiveness. Among the criteria that respondents are asked to use in making their assessments are the legislators' participation in committee work, their skill in guiding bills through floor debate, their expertise in special fields, the political power they hold (either by virtue of formal office, longevity, or personal attributes), and their ability to sway the opinion of their fellow legislators (NCCPPR 1978:4). An average effectiveness score is computed for each legislator based on survey results from each of the three respondent groups (i.e., legislators, lobbyists, and media). The effectiveness ratings for the North Carolina General Assembly from 1983, 1985, 1987, and 1989 are the dependent variables in this study. These four legislative sessions were selected because of the availability of data, and prior to 1983, three was the largest number of African Americans to serve in any one session of the assembly.

One advantage of using the North Carolina legislature as the object of analysis is the overall quality of the available data. For example, unlike the case in other states, the NCCPPR evaluations have only one dependent variable— effectiveness. Furthermore, a relatively recent study of the ratings methods and procedures used in various states concluded that the effectiveness analyses conducted by the NCCPPR are the most systematic, objective, and most widely respected (Mahtesian 1996).

Whatever the limitations of a single case, one case is clearly preferable to none at all. Moreover, here the shortcomings of the single-state sample are in part mitigated by the inclusion of data and analyses from multiple legislative sessions.[5] An additional advantage of using North Carolina's data is the fact that the legislature is in general not atypical of state legislatures for the time period studied. Although it is difficult to generalize about state legislatures, and "no state legislature can be said to 'represent' state legislatures in the sense of a sample representing the population" (Weissert 1989:17), it is important to note that on most dimensions, North Carolina's legislature does not differ significantly from other state legislatures.

> Like all other states (except Nebraska), it has two houses, and most of its legislators are male lawyers, businessmen, or farmers. Its members introduce approximately the same number of bills as the national average and give up their seats at approximately the same rate. Session length in North Carolina is typical of many states. Most or all [sic] members of the North Carolina legislature and the nation are part-timers, and like most states, have only very limited access to professional staff. . . . Salaries of North Carolina legislators are in the lower range, but not the lowest. And as in other states, the legislative agenda is dominated by spending issues for schools, highways, health care for the poor, welfare and a variety of judicial issues.[6] (Weissert 1989:17)

Table 5.1 gives the mean, standard deviation, and range for the dependent variable. These data reveal that the average overall effectiveness rating is relatively stable over the four sessions, and that there is considerable variation in effectiveness ratings with at least a 63-point spread between the most and least effective legislator in each of the sessions. Over the four-session period, twenty-five different African Americans served in the House, with only two of them appearing in all five sessions.

A pooled-analysis ordinary least squares (OLS) regression model is employed to examine the relative effects of race on perceptions of effectiveness. Pooling of the data has the virtue of providing a more substantial data base, and providing a single estimate for the effect of each independent variable over

TABLE 5.1

DESCRIPTIVE STATISTICS FOR THE DEPENDENT VARIABLE—
LEGISLATIVE EFFECTIVENESS

	1983	1985	1987	1989
Mean	45.9	44.6	45.1	46.0
Standard deviation	13.6	14.9	15.8	13.2
Range	22–90	20–90	19–93	22–85
No. of African Americans	11	13	14	13
N^*	116	115	116	110

$^*N$ = Number of legislators rated

the eight-year period. However, pooling does require assuming that the model is consistent across the years. To enhance that potential, I include dummy variables for *year* to allow for differences in evaluation across sessions caused by ebbs and flows in perceptions of effectiveness not captured by the independent variables in the model. More importantly, however, when sufficient data are present, I replicate the pooled analyses with session-specific analyses. These allow the more general pooled results to be directly compared with those of the specific sessions, eliminating any risk that information is lost or distortion occurs via pooling.[7]

Because each may be important in shaping one's perception of who is or is not an effective legislator, I include individual attribute, institutional position, and behavioral variables as controls. Specifically, the following variables, along with the race of the legislator, are included in the regression models.

FORMAL LEADERSHIP POSITIONS   Members who are part of the formal leadership are often viewed, by virtue of the powers inherent in their positions, as being more effective legislators than the rank and file. This is precisely the finding of studies by Meyer (1980) and Weissert (1989). Thus the expectation here is that being a formal leader is positively correlated to perceptions of effectiveness. Leadership positions include the speaker, majority and minority leaders, and chairs of each of the standing committees.

PARTY AFFILIATION   Because they are more likely to have their initiatives passed, and because they are more likely to hold formal leadership positions (e.g., Frantzich 1979; Hamm, Harmel, and Thompson 1983), it is reasonable to expect representatives from the majority party to be thought of as more effective. All the African Americans who served in the North Carolina General Assembly during the four sessions under investigation were Democrats. The Democratic Party was the majority party in each of the sessions.

SENIORITY   Seniority not only contributes to and enhances a member's expertise in certain policy matters, senior members also tend to be more knowledgeable of legislative rules and procedures. Therefore, they may be more effective in negotiating the legislative process (Meyer 1980; Weissert 1989). More senior members may also be more likely to hold leadership positions.

BILL INTRODUCTIONS   Proposing new laws is among the most basic functions that legislators perform. Bill introductions have often been used to gauge a representative's level of activity and to measure his or her commitment to their legislative responsibilities (Hamm, Harmel, and Thompson 1983; Haynie 1994; Rosenthal 1981). The expectation here is that the more bills legislators introduce, the more positively they will be perceived by their peers. Only substantive bills (i.e., bills that are intended to change the law or public policy) in which the legislator was a primary sponsor are counted as introductions. In other words, nonbinding resolutions and memorials were excluded from the analyses.

BEING AN ATTORNEY   In her study, Weissert (1989) found that being a lawyer had a significant impact on effectiveness. She argues that "serving as an attorney is particularly important since attorneys are trained in an area essential to the legislative process—bill drafting" (50). Because of this presumed skill in bill drafting, lawyers may be more active in bill introductions and, consequently, considered by their colleagues to be more effective legislators.

MEMBER OF THE APPROPRIATIONS OR RULES COMMITTEES   Legislative scholars have long recognized the importance of standing committees to the legislative process (e.g., Clapp 1963; Eulau and Karps 1977; Fenno 1973; Grier and Munger 1991; Rhode and Shepsle 1973; Stewart 1992). The conventional wisdom is that within a legislature, there are a small number of important committee assignments that are thought to confer power and influence to legislators. These assignments almost always include those committees that deal with appropriations, taxation, or budgeting, as well as the committees responsible for the rules that govern legislative procedure (Francis 1989; Smith and Deering 1984). Membership on these committees should enhance the perceived effectiveness of legislators.

RESULTS

One expectation suggested by the extant literature on racial attitudes was that (everything else being equal) African American legislators would be perceived as less effective than other representatives. The OLS regression results in table 5.2 suggest that this indeed was the case. The pooled results indicate that because of their race, African American legislators who served in the North Carolina House between 1983 and 1989 received effectiveness ratings from their peers that were, on average, 5.9 points lower than nonblack representatives. The separate year results provide additional evidence for the effect of race on African American legislators' reputations for effectiveness. Being African American

TABLE 5.2
REGRESSION ANALYSIS OF PERCEIVED LEGISLATIVE EFFECTIVENESS
(DEPENDENT VARIABLE = RATINGS BY *LEGISLATORS*)

Independent Variables	Pooled	1983	1985	1987	1989
Intercept	29.4**	24.6**	30.0**	22.7**	38.4**
	(1.3)	(2.2)	(1.7)	(1.9)	(3.4)
Race	−5.8**	−5.7*	−8.9**	−2.5	−8.3*
	(1.8)	(2.5)	(2.6)	(2.5)	(2.9)
Party	3.9**	9.3**	4.6**	5.2*	1.6
	(1.4)	(2.3)	(2.1)	(2.3)	(2.3)
Seniority	1.2**	1.6**	1.0**	1.7**	1.4*
	(.20)	(.37)	(.31)	(.39)	(.44)
Lawyer	9.2**	10.4**	9.0**	8.9**	10.1**
	(1.3)	(1.8)	(1.8)	(1.9)	(2.3)
Leadership	3.3**	3.3	3.2	5.3*	1.0
	(1.2)	(2.1)	(2.1)	(2.3)	(2.5)
Bill introductions	0.3**	0.2**	0.3**	0.3**	0.1
	(.05)	(.07)	(.07)	(.07)	(.09)
Rules committee	6.6**	6.9**	7.6**	5.1**	5.8*
	(1.1)	(1.7)	(1.6)	(1.8)	(2.2)
Appropriations Committee	0.9	0.5	1.8	0.3	−0.7
	(0.9)	(1.4)	(1.5)	(1.6)	(1.7)
Speaker	35.4**	31.8**	33.9**	33.8**	34.9**
	(2.4)	(7.8)	(8.4)	(9.5)	(8.4)
Year85	9.4	—	—	—	—
	(1.2)				
Year87	−2.0	—	—	—	—
	(1.1)				
Year89	2.2*	—	—	—	—
	(1.1)				
N	465	118	117	118	112.
Adjusted R²	.68	.72	.72	.74	.41

Note: Entries are unstandardized regression coefficients. Standard errors are in parentheses.

N = Number of legislators evaluated

**$p < .01$

*$p < .05$

TABLE 5.3

OLS REGRESSION OF PERCEIVED LEGISLATIVE
EFFECTIVENESS WITH INTERACTION TERMS

Independent Variables	B Values
Intercept	29.3**
	(1.4)
Race	−4.8
	(3.6)
Party	3.8**
	(1.5)
Seniority	1.3**
	(.21)
Lawyer	9.8**
	(1.5)
Leadership	3.8**
	(1.3)
Bill introductions	.28**
	(.06)
Rules Committee	6.1**
	(1.1)
Appropriations Committee	1.2
	(.98)
B senior	−1.4
	(1.2)
B lawyer	−2.6
	(2.5)
B leader	−2.1
	(3.5)
B intros	.21
	(.14)
B Rules Committee	5.8
	(3.8)
B Appropriations Committee	−1.4
	(2.9)
Year85	1.0
	(.79)
Year87	−1.9
	(1.1)
Year89	2.5
	(1.2)
N	464.
Adjusted R^2	.68

Note: Robust standard errors are in parentheses.

**$p < .01$

*$p < .05$

had a statistically significant negative effect in three of the four legislative sessions.

Our second hypothesis, which stated that due to the apparent decline in racist and discriminatory attitudes among whites, the race of African American legislators would have no impact on perceptions of their effectiveness, is obviously not supported by these results. These data show that racial considerations influenced evaluations of legislative behavior, and that these considerations had negative consequences for African American representatives.

The data in table 5.2 confirm that characteristics like holding leadership positions, having seniority, serving on prestigious committees, and being a lawyer are important contributors to perceptions of effectiveness. The third expectation posited that the race of the representative would have either a positive impact or no impact at all on how black legislators are evaluated when they possessed these characteristics. To test for this, I created six interaction terms that combined the race variable with each of the other independent variables and reran the pooled regression model (table 5.3).[8]

None of these six interaction terms had a statistically significant effect on perceptions of effectiveness. Being African American and a lawyer, African American and a leader, African American and more senior, and so on had no impact on the evaluations of black legislators. Thus, negative perceptions of black legislators appear not to be mitigated by their possessing characteristics that otherwise contribute to positive evaluations, and that tend to be sources of actual power and influence in legislatures.

Given the relatively small number of African Americans in each of the legislatures, it is possible that these apparent negative effects of race are due to the presence of a particularly ineffective African American legislator who is in the legislature throughout the entire period. To check for this possibility, I estimated additional pooled regression models, excluding the lowest-rated African American representative who served in all four legislative sessions. The results were not significantly different than those of the original models. Thus it is unlikely that the results reported here reflect some outlier effects.[9]

CONCLUSION

Based on the perceptions of their members, the data and analyses presented in this chapter suggest that state legislative institutions may not be as open to the participation and influence of African Americans as might otherwise appear.

The findings here provide evidence that, like African American political candidates in general, African Americans elected to state legislatures are perceived and evaluated negatively because of their race. Specifically, being black contributed to African American legislators in the North Carolina General Assembly being perceived by their colleagues as less effective than their nonblack peers. Moreover, the African American legislators did not reap any significant benefits from possessing characteristics and attributes that ordinarily enhance a legislator's reputation for effectiveness. That is, even when African American legislators were lawyers, members of the assembly's leadership, had seniority, or were in the majority party, they were still evaluated as less effective than other representatives.

These findings indicate that African American representatives are not viewed by their colleagues as equal participants in the deliberation and debate over matters of public policy. The classifications and racial considerations that abound in civic life appear to have also permeated important policy-making institutions. Consequently, policies and programs important to African American citizens may be less likely to receive serious consideration or enactment into law.

From a theoretical perspective, the findings here suggest that American political institutions are not race neutral or color-blind in their policy-making processes. If this is in fact the case, there are potentially serious implications for both the perceived and the de facto legitimacy of the governmental and representative process. I discuss this point in more detail in chapter 6.

CONCLUSION

This book has analytically examined several issues related to the nature and consequences of an African American presence in state legislatures. The preceding chapters have provided several empirical findings that should prove useful in future attempts to develop theories of African American elite behavior in general, and African American legislative behavior in particular. The overarching question guiding this study has been, what does it matter whether or not there are African Americans serving in state legislatures? In an effort to provide some initial answers to this question, this study has examined such issues as whether African American representatives have a noticeable and distinctive effect on state legislative agendas, whether they have achieved significant levels of incorporation and integration into the legislative process, and how African American legislators have been perceived by their peers. This concluding chapter summarizes the findings and discusses some of their implications for African American representation in state legislatures, as well as implications for African American politics more broadly speaking.

The book began with the proposition that African American legislators are the most prominent political examples and manifestations of W. E. B. Du Bois's duality dilemma. The argument is simply that any attempts to explain and understand the behavior of African American legislators and other black public officials must begin with a framework that takes into account that African

American representatives are expected to simultaneously be what St. Clair Drake and Horace Cayton (1945) called race representatives and what Nicholas Masters (1961) labeled "responsible legislators." That is, we need to be cognizant of the fact that the behavior of African American legislators is shaped, to a significant degree, by the pressures that arise as they undertake the precarious and difficult task of becoming incorporated into legislative institutions, while at the same time trying to transform these institutions and the policies that they produce. This requires that we not simply note the existence of the duality dilemma as many prior studies have done, but that we actively integrate the implications of its existence into our explanations of political behavior.

While all legislators at times must contend with competing or conflicting demands from various constituency groups, I have suggested that these pressures are not as profound as those associated with the duality dilemmas faced by African Americans. The facts and circumstances related to how African Americans first came to be in North America, the experiences of confronting pervasive and entrenched beliefs in the inherent inferiority of black people, a long history of de jure and de facto discrimination and segregation, and the reoccurring general economic subjugation and political disenfranchisement of blacks—together these factors have contributed to both the creation and perpetuation of an omnipresent feeling of alienation from the larger American society, and the stimulation and reinforcement of strong racial group identity within the African American community (e.g., Anderson 1997; Dawson 1994; Massey and Denton 1993; Morris 1984; Pinderhughes 1987). Both of these considerations (i.e., the widespread alienation and strong racial group identity) are key components in what Michael Dawson (1994) calls the "black utility heuristic." Dawson's black utility heuristic is the phenomenon of individual African Americans using their perception of the condition of African Americans as a group as a proxy for their own personal standing (Dawson 1994:61). In other words, there is a tendency for "African Americans [to] evaluate events not only as Americans but also as a group that has been historically exploited in American society" (161–62). African American elites and elected officials are likely to share this strong sense of racial identity, which often places them in situations where they must choose between being race representatives or so-called "responsible legislators." The pressures for non-African American representatives, both men and women, to address and satisfy conflicting or competing demands rarely, if ever, results in the "double-consciousness" that is so often a consequence for African Americans.[1] If and when it exists, the need for non-African Americans to be race or gender representatives is episodic or temporary.

This process is [for African Americans], in many respects, similar to what the Irish, Jews, Italians, and other ethnic groups have undergone. All of these groups have had their race men [and women] at certain times in their histories, but as the groups' fortunes have risen, the need for their respective race men [and women] has declined and other individuals have emerged who are increasingly more interested in their professions and class positions. These individuals don't necessarily forget their roots, but often the needs of the profession win out, and class issues take precedence over public displays of ethnic and racial particularism. This is what we have come to expect as a normal consequence of upward mobility in the United States. *The exception is that of race and the nature and complexity of racism that blacks face.*

(Anderson 1997:118; emphasis added)

The "new black politics" era, which began in the mid-1960s, is most noted for the movement of African American political behavior away from an almost exclusive reliance on pressure or protest politics toward a much greater reliance on electoral participation. It is clear that these changes reconfigured the appearance of American political institutions. This transition in African American political behavior contributed to a monumental growth in the number of African American elected officials at all levels of government. Yet the mere presence of black faces in public policy-making institutions was never intended to be an end unto itself. Rather, the hope was that the inclusion of African Americans would lead to tangible substantive outcomes and benefits for black people.

The civil rights movement began as an effort to secure the most basic political rights—the right to vote and the right to equal treatment before the law—but rapidly expanded in scope to demand governmental action to end discrimination in employment, public education, housing, and public facilities generally and to alleviate poverty and reduce unemployment, expand health care to blacks and other low-income groups, and gain other government benefits.[2]   (Browning, Marshall, and Tabb 1984:2)

The evidence reported in this book indicates that the presence and growth of African American representation in government has indeed had noticeable and meaningful policy consequences. I have shown that there is a powerful and significant connection between descriptive and substantive representation. African American state legislators tend to provide much more than window dressing or diversity for diversity's sake. Among other things, they provide substantive representation of black interests. The data and analyses presented in this book clearly challenge Carol Swain's conclusion that "descriptive representation of blacks only guarantees black faces and is, at best, an intangible good; [while] substantive representation is by definition real and color blind" (Swain 1993:211).

A DISTINCTIVE IMPACT?

The emergence and growth of an African American presence in state legislatures in the aftermath of the civil rights struggles of the 1960s was accompanied by widespread expectations that black legislators would introduce to these institutions issues of particular importance to African American citizens. That is, African American legislators have been expected, first and foremost, to be "race representatives." They have been expected to provide African American citizens with substantive representation by primarily articulating and supporting a black interest agenda.

Has this expectation been met? Based on the analyses and findings in this volume, the answer to this question is not a simple yes or no. It is clear that, in comparison with nonblack legislators, African American legislators did pursue a distinctive set of legislative issues. African Americans were the primary advocates for black interests in each of the five state legislatures examined in this study. Specifically, I found that African American legislators were twice as likely as nonblack legislators to introduce black interest legislation. Also, a majority of African American legislators introduced black interest legislation in all of the legislative sessions. In contrast, in only one of the fifteen sessions did the total number of nonblack representatives who introduced at least one black interest bill exceed 25 percent.

Similarly, in their committee assignments, black representatives tended to accumulate more power and acquire more influence in black interest policy areas than in any other area. Using two separate measures—*saliency*, measured as the percentage of all African American committee assignments devoted to a particular type of committee, and *influence potential*, calculated as the percentage of a committee's membership that is African American—I found that African American legislators were well positioned on standing committees to advance or protect a black interest agenda. For all three legislative sessions in four of the five states, a black interest committee was among the top two committees in terms of potential African American influence.

While it is true that the African American representatives added a distinctive race-based agenda to the policy debates within state legislatures, it is also true that they demonstrated interest in issues with no apparent racial content as well. In chapter 1, in addition to the race representative option, I identified two alternative strategies available to black representatives for maneuvering or managing the challenges resulting from the double-consciousness or duality dilemmas that they experience in performing their professional duties. One of these was deracialization. With deracialization, African American lawmakers purposefully choose to eliminate or de-emphasize issues in their legislative agendas that may be viewed in explicitly racial terms, and they emphasize those issues that are not race-specific and that appeal to a broader constituency (Barker and Jones 1994; McCormick 1989). Such behavior is consistent with what is expected of "responsible legislators." The second alternative strategy was a type of middle-ground tactic that combines elements of both the race representative and the deracialization approaches. With this strategy, what Canon (1999) has labeled the "balancing perspective," African American legislators recognize the significance of racial differences and they perhaps make race-related matters their top priority, but they also give attention to issues of broader concern and that have no specific racial content.

The findings presented in the preceding chapters suggest that the behavior of African American state legislators is most characteristic of the middle-ground or balancing perspective. It is clear that in favoring black interests in their agenda-setting activities and their committee assignments, African American legislators behaved in a manner that typifies the race representative. Yet the data and analyses also show that these representatives concerned themselves with other policy matters that were not necessarily or directly related to race. For example, although African American lawmakers were twice as likely as non-African Americans to introduce black interest bills, these were not the only types of bills that they introduced. In fact, in only two of the fourteen legislative sessions did black interest legislation make up a majority of the collective bill introductions of the African American legislators.[3] Likewise, black interest committees were the most salient committee assignments for black legislators, and they were the committees on which African Americans tended to have the most influence potential. However, over time, there was increased diversification in the committee assignment patterns of the black legislators to include more assignments on nonrace-related committees. Thus in their bill introductions and their standing committee service, the African American legislators seemed to behave *both* as race representatives *and* "responsible legislators"—balancing their concern for black interests with their concern for other interests of importance to their districts, their legislative careers, or to both.

AFRICAN AMERICAN POLITICAL INCORPORATION

Political incorporation refers to the extent to which a group is strategically positioned within political institutions to exercise significant influence over the policy-making process (Browning, Marshall, and Tabb 1984). For cohesive legislative subgroups like African Americans, political incorporation is seen as an important precondition to having a meaningful effect on government policies and programs. The argument is that political incorporation is a better predictor of policy responsiveness than descriptive representation alone, and that higher levels of incorporation place groups in a more advantageous position to insure that the interests with which they are concerned are heard and seriously considered during the decision-making process (Browning, Marshall, and Tabb 1984; Sonenshein 1993). Using an incorporation index designed especially for the legislative environment, I found that African American political incorporation in state legislatures has grown dramatically since the mid-1970s.

In terms of the relationship between political incorporation and governmental responsiveness to African American legislators and black interests, the findings reported here indicate that higher levels of African American incorporation do not necessarily translate into what I called internal responsiveness. There was a negative and statistically insignificant relationship between black political incorporation and the passage rates of bills introduced by African American representatives. However, with regard to what I referred to as external responsiveness—state spending in black interest policy categories—political incorporation was found to have a positive effect. In general, the higher the level of African American incorporation, the more states spent on health, education, and social welfare programs.

Surprisingly, and contrary to the findings of previous studies of minority-group political incorporation, the evidence reported in this book indicates that the effects of higher levels of African American incorporation were not decidedly superior to the effects of increased African American descriptive representation. Although black political incorporation had positive and significant effects on spending in each of the black interest policy areas, it was also the case that just the presence of African Americans in state legislatures, regardless of their political incorporation status, was sufficient to yield significant governmental responsiveness to these interests. In other words, African Americans seem to benefit almost as much from the simple presence of blacks in state legislatures as they do from high levels of African American incorporation in these same institutions.

In the Eyes of Their Peers

Whether African American legislators are ultimately successful in their legislative endeavors depends, to a significant degree, on how they are perceived by their colleagues in the legislature. Evidence presented in this book suggests that, everything else being equal, black legislators are perceived and evaluated negatively by other legislators. The case study that examined perceptions of legislative effectiveness in the North Carolina General Assembly yielded the conclusion that their race contributed to African American legislators' being perceived as less effective than their nonblack peers. Even when the African American legislators possessed the characteristics and attributes that, according to previous studies, ordinarily enhance a legislator's reputation for effectiveness, they were nevertheless viewed negatively. In other words, when African American legislators were lawyers, members of the assembly leadership, had seniority, and/or were in the majority party, they were still perceived as less effective than other representatives.

These findings are seemingly at odds with what we have learned about African American political incorporation in state legislatures. The political incorporation index utilizes measures such as seniority, standing committee assignments, majority party membership, and leadership positions to assess the status and clout of the black lawmakers. When their power and influence potential were assessed using this more or less objective scale, the African American legislators in this study fared fairly well. Their level of political incorporation increased significantly from one decade to the next in each of the five states. On the other hand, when judged by the much more subjective standard of perceived legislative effectiveness, the black legislators seemed to be decidedly disadvantaged. Consequently, these findings, notwithstanding what we already know about African American political incorporation, raise interesting and important questions about the openness of state legislative institutions to meaningful participation and influence from African Americans. If, all else being equal, African American representatives are deemed by their peers to be less effective than nonblack legislators, how successful can they really be in changing or shaping the policies that state legislatures produce?

IMPLICATIONS

At the outset of this book I indicated that the answers to the questions that were to be addressed were potentially relevant to democratic theory and that they had some normative implications for our system of representative government and for African American politics. With regard to African American politics, Lucius Barker and Mack Jones (1994), in one of the more popular texts on the subject, criticized contemporary African American politics for becoming too "routinized." They argued that as African American elected officials have gradually become more integrated or incorporated into political institutions, they seem to place less emphasis and importance on race and the advocacy of black interests. As a consequence of this routinization, they argue, black representatives' behavior in these institutions has become conventional, in "more of a *system supporting* than a *system challenging* fashion" (322; emphasis in original). For example, Barker and Jones write:

> Seeking to retain a viable political force, the national Democratic Party has followed its erstwhile white supporters to the political right and, in order to remain within the mainstream of the Democratic Party, black political operatives have also moved toward the conservative center, de-emphasizing in the process race-specific interests.   (1994:323)

They go on to say that if this trend of routinization continues, it will likely lead to a state of affairs in African American politics where "there will be no agenda that directly addresses the key issues and concerns of blacks, and no effective structures through which one could be forged" (324).

With this argument, Barker and Jones are expressing the long and widely held fear in African American politics that "working within the system," or so-called "cross-over strategies"—attempts by African American officeholders or candidates for public office to cultivate support from or enter into coalitions with nonblacks—necessarily mean the abandonment of a black interest or progressive agenda. Although I did not directly address this specific issue, some of the results in this book do, however, speak to this concern.

I have presented findings which quite clearly indicate that the fears expressed by Barker and Jones, among others (e.g., Walters 1992), may be in large part unfounded, or at least exaggerated. Being a race representative and a "responsible legislator" is not necessarily an either-or proposition. For the African American legislators in the five states studied here, it seemed to have been "both-and" rather than "either-or." That is, they tended to provide strong advocacy and support for black interests as well as demonstrate concern for other nonrace-related issues that may have been important to their broader constituency, their legislative careers, or to both. My findings in this regard are consistent with the principles expressed in David Canon's (1999) "balancing commonality" perspective, which allows for the creation of biracial or multiracial coalitions, "but within the context of serving black interests as well" (254).

In terms of implications for democratic theory, one of the core tenets of our representative democracy is that the substantive interests that exist in the politic be represented through deliberation (Bessette 1994; Manin 1997; Mansbridge 1999). Whether such substantive representation depends upon descriptive representation is one of the questions addressed in a recent article by Jane Mansbridge (1999). According to Mansbridge and other normative theorists (e.g., Bessette 1994; Gutman and Thompson 1996), the answer to this question is yes. Mansbridge argues that descriptive representation is all but essential to the deliberative functions of representative democracy (629). The deliberative function serves to determine which policies are good for a representative's constituency, and which policies benefit the polity as a whole. "It also aims at transforming interests and creating commonality when that commonality can be genuinely good for all. In its deliberative function, a representative body should ideally include at least one representative who can speak for every group that might provide new information, perspectives, or ongoing insights relevant to the understanding that leads to a decision" (634). In other words, a diverse and varied set of ideas contributes to a deliberation that is healthy for a democracy, and the best way to get this diversity and variety is to have a diverse group of representatives in deliberative institutions like legislatures. Ever since the founding of the American republic, race, ethnicity, and gender have been the diversities that have been most salient and the ones that have mattered the most.

With regard to black interests, the empirical findings here indicate that these are indeed more likely to be introduced and deliberated in state legislatures when there are African American representatives present. The data and analyses in the preceding chapters demonstrate that there is a strong connection between the race of the representative and the type of representation African American constituents receive.[4] That is, African American legislators are, for the most part, the ones who speak for African Americans and black interests in state legislatures. It is not possible to say definitively what nonblack legislators would or would not do in their absence, but we do know that when African Americans are present, they are the ones most likely to introduce, for debate, deliberation, and possible enactment, issues of particular concern and importance to the larger African American community.

A continued basic level of trust in our political institutions and the continued legitimacy of our current representative system may rest in part on our ability to insure that there are significant numbers of African Americans (as well as women and other minority groups) in deliberative institutions who speak with distinctive African American (or female or other minority-group) voices.[5] Moreover, once inside these institutions, we must seek to insure that these representatives are perceived and treated as equal participants, and that their ideas and views are seriously considered. This task is becoming increasingly urgent, given the rapid demographic changes that the United States is currently undergoing. Historically disadvantaged and disenfranchised groups, such as African Americans, are quickly becoming a much larger proportion of this country's population. For the health of our democracy, decision-making institutions must be accessible and open to influence from such groups. As Mansbridge puts it, "Seeing proportional numbers of members of their group exercising the responsibility of ruling with full status in the legislature can enhance de facto legitimacy by making citizens, and particularly members of historically underrepresented groups, feel as if they themselves were present in the deliberations."[6]

APPENDIX

APPENDIX TO CHAPTER 3

BLACK INTEREST COMMITTEES IN THE FIVE STATES

Arkansas	Illinois	Maryland	New Jersey	North Carolina
Joint Committee on Youth and Children	Cities and Villages	Constitutional and Administrative Law	Community Development and Urban Affairs	Education
Education	Education	Judiciary	Education	Election Laws
Judiciary	Elections	Ways and Means	Higher Education	Higher Education
Public Health, Welfare, and Labor	Higher Education		Housing	Judiciary I, II, III
	Judiciary		Institutions and Welfare	Public Welfare
	Public Welfare and Human Resources		Judiciary	
	Urban Development			

PRESTIGE COMMITTEES IN THE FIVE STATES

Arkansas	Illinois	Maryland	New Jersey	North Carolina
Revenue and Taxation	Appropriations	Appropriations	Appropriations	Appropriations
Rules	Revenue	Rules and Executive Nominations	Taxation	Budget
Joint Budget	Rules		Rules and Order	Finance
			Ways and Means	Rules and Operation of the House

POLICY COMMITTEES IN THE FIVE STATES

Arkansas	Illinois	Maryland	New Jersey	North Carolina
Insurance and Commerce	Banks and Savings & Loans	(None)	Banking and Insurance	Alcoholic Beverage Control
Public Transportation	Highways and Traffic Safety		Law, Public Safety and Defense	Banking and Banks
Joint Committee on Energy	Insurance		Transportation and Public Utilities	Commerce
	Public Utilities			Corporations
	Registration and Regulation			Correctional Institutions
				Courts and Judicial Districts
				Economy
				Highway Safety
				Insurance
				Law Enforcement
				Public Utilities
				Roads and Transportation
				UNC Board of Governors

CONSTITUENCY COMMITTEES IN THE FIVE STATES

Arkansas	Illinois	Maryland	New Jersey	North Carolina
Aging and Legislative Affairs	Agriculture	Economic Matters	Agriculture	Aging
Agriculture and Economic Development	Conservation and Water	Environmental Matters	Air and Water Pollution and Public Health	Commercial Fisheries
City, County, and Local Affairs	Consumer Protection		County and Municipal Government	Conservation and Development
Economic & Industrial Resources and Development	County and Township Affairs		Energy and Natural Resources	Employment Security
Joint Committee on Public Retirement and Social Security	Environment, Energy, and Natural Resources		Environmental Quality	Local Government (I, II)
	Industry and Labor Relations		Labor Relations	Manufacturers and Labor
	Labor and Commerce		Senior Citizens	Mental Health
	Municipalities		Solid Waste Management	Military Affairs
	Veterans Affairs		Transportation and Public Utilities	Natural and Economic Resources
			Veteran Affairs	Wildlife Resources

NOTES

1. INTRODUCTION: RACE REPRESENTATIVES OR "RESPONSIBLE LEGISLATORS"?

1. *Dred Scott v. Sanford,* 60 U.S. 393, 19 Howard 393 (1857).

2. See for example, Lucius Barker and Mack Jones, *African Americans and the American Political System,* 353–60; Charles V. Hamilton, "Deracialization: Examination of a Political Strategy," 3–5; Joseph P. McCormick II and Charles E. Jones, "The Conceptualization of Deracialization," 79; and Katherine Tate, *From Protest to Politics: The New Black Voters in American Elections,* ch. 1.

3. Norman Beckman, "U.S. Budget Shifts Costs to States," 12–13; Charles A. Bowsher, "Federal Cutbacks Strengthen State Role," 18–21; and Nathan and Doolittle, "The Evolution of Federal Aid."

4. St. Clair Drake and Horace Cayton, *Black Metropolis.* For a succinct discussion of the race man concept, see Elijah Anderson's "The Precarious Balance: Race Man or Sellout?" in Ellis Cose, ed., *The Darden Dilemma,* 114–32.

5. See Dymally (1971) for a similar view.

6. Friedman 1993:30. The group of legislators that Friedman alludes to includes women and African Americans.

7. Button and Scher (1984) discuss a related concept that they call "the problem of dual legitimacy." The dilemma associated with dual legitimacy stems from the

fact that African American officials elected to local offices often run in at-large electoral systems. Button and Scher argue that, in this context, black candidates need "to appeal to whites as well as blacks in order to win and stay in office, and therefore they are less committed to serving blacks" (211).

8. This phenomenon is often referred to as "double-consciousness."

9. The race representative and the deracialization strategies involved are akin to David Canon's (1995, 1999) difference and commonality perspectives, respectively. According to Canon, difference representatives consider themselves first and foremost as advocates for African American constituents, while commonality representatives downplay the racial aspects of political issues. See Canon 1995:161–64, and 1999:34–46.

10. McCormick and Jones (1993) point out that deracialization can be used as an electoral as well as an agenda-setting strategy. As an electoral strategy, deracialization is "connected with attempts to capture office in majority white political jurisdictions," and as an agenda-setting strategy, it is "connected with governance after elections have been won" (69).

11. Wilson 1987:162. It is important to note that Wilson's advocacy for "universal" programs does not completely remove racial considerations from the policy process. It simply relegates to race a less prominent role. He writes, for example, "I emphasized that although this program would include targeted strategies—both means tested and race-specific—they would be considered secondary to the universal program so that the latter are seen as the most visible and dominant aspects in the eyes of the general public" (162).

12. The lone exception is the data used in chapter 5. A detailed discussion of these data may be found there.

13. The regional diversity accounted for here is the South (Arkansas and North Carolina), the Mid-Atlantic (Maryland), the Midwest (Illinois), and the Northeast (New Jersey).

2. AGENDA-SETTING AND THE REPRESENTATION OF BLACK INTERESTS

1. Pitkin, The Concept of Representation, 209–211. Also see Heinz Eulau and Paul D. Karps, "The Puzzle of Representation: Specifying Components of Responsiveness," Legislative Studies Quarterly 2 (August): 3.

2. Blue quoted in Van Denton, "N.C. Blacks Stand to Make Big Political Gains," Raleigh News and Observer, October 4, 1962, 1A. Representative Blue, a Democrat from Wake County, is the first and only African American to be selected speaker of the North Carolina General Assembly.

3. See Jewell (1983) for a detailed review of the major literature on legislative-constituency relations.

4. Seventy-six percent of the African American representatives included in this study were elected in majority black districts. Similarly, Button and Hedge (1993) found that 75 percent of black state legislators responding to their national survey represented majority black districts.

5. See Dawson 1994, esp. 10–11, 45–48.

6. See W. B. Gallie, "Essentially Contested Concepts," in Max Black, ed. *The Importance of Language.*

7. Although table 2.3 only shows data for selected years between 1970 and 1990, U.S. census data confirms this assertion. See U.S. Department of Commerce 1991: table 717.

8. Gurin, Hatchett, and Jackson's (1989) finding that there is a general congruence between the policy preferences of African Americans of various social classes is consistent with the findings of an earlier, though less comprehensive, study by Ippolito, Donaldson, and Bowman (1968).

9. Also see Tate (1993) who reports similar findings regarding the policy preferences of African Americans.

10. See also Richard L. Hall, *Participation in Congress,* and Richard L. Hall and Frank W. Wayman, "Buying Time: Moneyed Interests and the Mobilization of Bias in Congressional Committees," *American Political Science Review* 84:797–820, for similar discussions of the problems relative to the use of roll calls as reflections of legislative behavior.

11. The data used here are from an original data-set constructed by Kathleen A. Bratton and myself. Much of the analysis in this chapter is drawn from Bratton and Haynie (1992, 1999a).

12. Only "substantive" bill introductions are used in this analysis. Substantive bills are proposals for new laws or programs. Nonbinding resolutions and memorials are not counted as bill introductions for this study. For New Jersey, bills introduced in 1978 and 1988 were included rather than bills introduced in 1979 and 1989. Legislative elections were held in 1977 and 1987, and the following years were the ones in which newly elected representatives could reasonably be expected to have some impact in the legislature.

13. As used in this table, black interest bills include introductions concerning civil rights, education, health care, poverty/social welfare as well as children's and women's issues. The percentages are based on data pooled from each of the five states.

14. Dummy variables are included to control for state effects, omitting New Jersey as a reference category. Likewise, dummy variables were used to control for year effects, omitting 1969 as a reference category.

15. See, for example, Bratton and Haynie (1999a), who find that women are more likely than men to introduce black interest legislation.

16. The majority black district variable is a dichotomous variable coded 1 if the district is majority black and 0 otherwise.

17. As with Herring (1990), the population of the largest city in the district logged is used to measure urbanness.

18. It should be noted that both the Swain and Whitby studies focused on the representation of African American interests at the congressional level, whereas this chapter examines black interest representation in state legislatures.

19. *Miller v. Johnson*, 515 U.S. 900 (1995); *Bush v. Vera*, 517 U.S. 952 (1996). For analysis and commentary on these and similar U.S. Supreme Court cases, see Canon 1999:60–92, and Reeves 1997.

20. This finding was first reported in Bratton and Haynie 1999a.

3. RACE, REPRESENTATION, AND COMMITTEE ASSIGNMENTS

1. For example, see Charles L. Clapp, *The Congressman: His Job As He Sees It;* Richard Fenno, *The Power of the Purse: Appropriations Politics in Congress* and *Congressmen in Committees;* Wayne L. Francis, *The Legislative Committee Game: A Comparative Analysis of Fifty States;* George Goodwin, *The Little Legislatures: Committees of Congress;* Kevin B. Grier and Michael C. Munger, "Committee Assignments, Constituent Preferences, and Campaign Contributions"; Kenneth A. Shepsle, "Congressional Committee Assignments: An Optimization Model with Institutional Constraints" and "Representation and Governance: The Great Trade-off"; Steven Smith and Christopher Deering, *Committees in Congress;* and Charles Stewart, "Committee Hierarchies in the Modernizing House, 1875–1947."

2. Francis (1989) cautions that we can only assume truthfulness in the survey respondents' answers. He warns that "it is possible . . . that legislators tempered their committee assignment request to match their expectations of success in receiving those assignments" (26–27). Also see Shepsle 1978, chs. 3–5, for an in-depth discussion and treatment of this point.

3. See chapter 2 for a more detailed discussion defining black interests.

4. In the mid-1960s, as the most blatant forms of racial discrimination begin to dissipate and African Americans begin to enjoy political enfranchisement, emphasis began to shift toward improving the conditions of the nation's poor with President Lyndon Johnson's War on Poverty and Great Society programs. Particular attention was given to the African American community as a result of studies like Daniel Patrick Moynihan's *The Negro Family* (1965).

5. Eulau identifies Rhode and Shepsle (1973) as an example of a study with this particular flaw.

6. Canon (1999) has an excellent discussion and provides in-depth analyses of this general point (see esp. 34–59 and ch. 4).

7. The total number of African American committee assignments is arrived at by aggregating all the committee assignments held by each individual African American legislator in a legislative session.

8. The political incorporation of African Americans in state legislatures is dealt with more fully in chapter 4.

9. Such politicians are also referred to as representatives of the "new black politics." For example, see Barker and Jones (1994:322).

10. In contrast to the commonality representatives are what Canon (1999) calls "difference" representatives. Difference representatives are quite similar to the race representatives described in this study. They "view politics through the lens of race and require representation of distinctive black interest by black representatives" (39).

11. This measure may, in many instances, underestimate the true influence potential of black legislators on standing committees. For example, African Americans are certain to have more influence on a committee when their party is in the majority than when it is not.

12. There were no African Americans in the Arkansas House in 1969.

13. Urban affairs issues fell within the jurisdiction of the Cities and Villages Committee in 1979.

14. In Maryland, the Ways and Means Committee is categorized as a black interest committee rather than a prestige committee because it handles education, health, and social welfare matters.

15. Specifically, Bratton and Haynie (1999b) found that "in Illinois, blacks are significantly more likely than whites to serve on all three types of committees; in North Carolina, blacks are significantly more likely to serve on education and welfare committees; and in New Jersey blacks are significantly more likely than whites to serve on welfare committees" (13). They report similar findings for women legislators.

4. AFRICAN AMERICAN POLITICAL INCORPORATION: A VIEW FROM THE STATES

1. See, for example, Barker and Jones, *African Americans and the American Political System*, 321–30; Hamilton, "Deracialization: Examination of a Political Strate-

gy," 3–5; McCormick and Jones, "The Conceptualization of Deracialization," 79; and Tate, *From Protest to Politics,* ch. 1.

2. Although Bobo and Gilliam (1990) use the term "political empowerment" rather than political incorporation, they are characterizing a set of processes and conditions almost identical to the ones described here and by Browning, Marshall, and Tabb 1984.

3. Prestige or power committees are the Appropriations, Budget, Finance/Taxation, and Rules committees (see Smith and Deering 1980:84). Leadership positions include assistant majority/minority leader, party whips, assistant party whips, and committee chairs. The Speaker, majority leader, and minority leader positions are counted separately.

4. For examples of studies that examine variables or characteristics that contribute to power and influence in legislatures, see Heinz Eulaum "Bases of Authority in Legislative Bodies: A Comparative Analysis"; Stephen Frantzich, "Who Makes Our Laws? The Legislative Effectiveness of Members of the U.S. Congress"; Keith E. Hamm, Robert Harmel, and Robert Thompson, "Ethnic and Partisan Minorities in Two Southern Legislatures"; Kerry L. Haynie, "The Color of Their Skin or the Content of Their Behavior?"; Malcom E. Jewell, *The State Legislature;* Katherine Meyer, "Legislative Influence: Toward Theory Development Through Causal Analysis"; David M. Olson and Cynthia T. Nonidez, "Measures of Legislative Performance in the U.S. House of Representatives"; and Carol S. Weissert, "Determinants and Dynamics of Perceived Legislative Effectiveness in the North Carolina State Legislature, 1977–1987."

5. African Americans' presence in state legislatures dates back to Reconstruction, but my usage of "new" here refers to the reemergence of African American representation in state legislatures in the post-1950s and during the civil rights movement of the 1960s.

6. The fifteen legislative sessions (five states, three time points) were divided into quartiles for the purposes of the analyses that follow. Because fifteen does not divide evenly by four, the "highest" quartile contains just three sessions.

7. Frantzich 1979:411. See Dahl (1956, 1961) for similar and related arguments.

8. For examples of alternative explanations for legislative decision-making, see R. Douglas Arnold, *The Logic of Congressional Action;* Morris Fiorina, *Congress: Keystone of the Washington Establishment;* Kingdon 1981; and David R. Mayhew, *Congress: The Electoral Connection.*

9. The result for African American political incorporation is particularly surprising given how the concept is measured. Recall that the incorporation scale includes measures for seniority, leadership positions, majority party status, and prestige committee assignments. These characteristics have often been found to be positively related to legislators' ability to successfully guide bills through the legisla-

tive labyrinth (e.g., Bratton and Haynie 1999a, 1999b; Frantzich 1979; Haynie 1999; Hibbing 1991, 1993; Jacobson 1992). For example, Bratton and Haynie (1999a), in a study that includes all the states and each of the legislative sessions examined here, found that being in the majority party and holding leadership positions contributed to a legislator's success at passing bills.

10. This finding is similar to the findings of the 45-state study of political incorporation conducted by Nelson (1991:14).

11. The claim regarding African American citizens' desire for more government spending for education is supported by several studies of African American public opinion. See, for example, Dawson 1994; Gurin, Hatchett, and Jackson 1989; and Keene et al. 1993.

12. Ideally, a time-series approach should be used, but such an analysis is not possible with the present data set.

13. For an in-depth discussion of each of these variables' (and others') potential impact on state spending decisions, see Paul E. Peterson, *The Price of Federalism*, 89–103.

14. It should be noted, however, that my incorporation index differs significantly from Nelson's in that it measures political incorporation using a broader perspective.

5. RACE AND PEER EVALUATIONS OF AFRICAN AMERICAN LEGISLATORS: A CASE STUDY

1. In the extant literature, this category has not included race, class, or gender. Instead, it has been a proxy for such characteristics as party affiliation, educational level, and occupational background.

2. Meyer (1980) and Weissert (1989) present a more detailed discussion of this literature and its uses of these variables. See Hall (1992) for a general critique of these studies.

3. It should be noted that some studies (e.g., Citrin, Green, and Sears 1990; Sigelman et al. 1995) argue that there are certain conditions under which race is not a critical factor in how black political candidates are evaluated.

4. See Charles Mahtesian, "Best and Dimmest," for a more detailed review and evaluation of these and other effectiveness studies.

5. For a similar use of this method and approach in a one-state study using NCCPPR's effectiveness data, see Carol S. Weissert, "Issue Salience and State Legislative Effectiveness" (1991).

6. In two respects, the North Carolina legislature was somewhat atypical for the period studied. North Carolina's legislature had more standing committees than

any other state, and it experienced one-party dominance. The limited party competition was typical of some Southern states, but not the nation as a whole (Weissert 1989).

7. The pooled data structure is unusual in that it includes many legislators multiple times, but is not generally a panel design. A representative could appear one, two, three, four, or five times in the pooling, depending on the number of sessions in which he or she served. In fact, all these possibilities are present in the data, with just thirty-eight legislators (two African Americans) appearing in all five sessions. The repeat appearance of legislators introduces serial correlation. In general, OLS is unbiased, though inefficient, in the face of either serial correlation or heteroskedasticity. With the number of units in each cross section considerably larger than the number of time points, there should be no serious loss in efficiency in the estimates. OLS standard errors are, however, suspect and will be underestimated.

For the pooled analyses in regression tables, I report robust standard errors with an additional correction for multiple observations per legislator (Rogers 1993; White 1980). Thus both individual legislator effects, to account for serial correlation, and any heteroskedastic effects are incorporated in the estimated standard errors.

8. The specific interactive variables created and assessed are: African American x Seniority, African American x Leadership, African American x Lawyer, African American x Rules Committee, African American x Appropriations Committee, and African American x Bill Introductions.

9. Because the results of these additional regression models are not significantly different from what is reported above, I do not include them in the text.

6. CONCLUSION

1. Although it is true that women legislators sometimes face similar dilemmas, the pressures to focus on women's issues seems not to be as great for them as the pressures for African Americans to focus on black interests. This may be due to the fact that there tend to be more women than African Americans in legislatures, and the fact that, in any given legislature, women legislators as a group are more diverse ideologically and are less cohesive than African Americans. See, for example, Carroll 1991:3.

2. Also see Barker and Jones (1994:353–60) for a similar view.

3. There was a total of fifteen legislative sessions examined in this book (five states and three sessions each), but there were no African Americans in the Arkansas legislature in 1969; thus only fourteen of the legislative sessions are considered here.

4. Canon (1995, 1999) and Whitby (1997) offer three studies on race and repre-

sentation in the U.S. Congress that reach conclusions similar to the ones I reach here regarding the link between descriptive and substantive representation. For a brief summary of their conclusions, see the discussion of Whitby's *The Color of Representation* and Canon's *Race, Redistricting, and Representation* at the end of chapter 2 of the present volume.

5. There is much debate about what exactly constitutes "significant numbers." Mansbridge (1999) makes a persuasive argument in favor of proportional representation. She writes, "In practice, . . . disadvantaged groups often need the full representation that proportionality allows in order to achieve several goals: deliberative synergy, critical mass, dispersion of influence, and a range of views within the group" (636). She goes on to say that "the demand for proportionality is accentuated by the fact that, in practice, almost all democratic assemblies are aggregative as well as deliberative, and achieving the full normative legitimacy of the aggregative function requires that the members of the representative body cast votes for each affected conflicting interest in proportion to the numbers of such interest bearers in the population" (637).

6. Mansbridge 1999:650. See Guinier 1994 for a similar argument.

BIBLIOGRAPHY

Advisory Commission on Intergovernmental Relations. 1982. *Tax Capacity of the 50 States: Methodology and Estimates.* Washington, D.C.: Advisory Commission on Intergovernmental Relations.

———. 1992. *Significant Features of Fiscal Federalism.* Vol. 2. Washington, D.C.: Advisory Commission on Intergovernmental Relations.

Anderson, Elijah. 1997. "The Precarious Balance: Race Man or Sellout?" In Ellis Cose, ed., *The Darden Dilemma,* 114–32. New York: Harper Perennial.

Arnold, R. Douglas. 1990. *The Logic of Congressional Action.* New Haven: Yale University Press.

Asher, Herbert B. 1975. "The Changing Status of the Freshmen Representative." In Norman J. Ornstein, ed., *Congress in Change,* 216–39. New York: Praeger.

Baker, S. and P. Kleppner. 1986. "Race War Chicago Style: The Election of a Black Mayor." In T. N. Clark, ed., *Research in Urban Policy.* Vol. 2. Greenwich, Conn.: JAI Press.

Barker, Lucius and Mack Jones. 1994. *African Americans and the American Political System.* 4th ed. Englewood Cliffs, N.J.: Prentice-Hall.

Barnett, Margurite Ross. 1975. "The Congressional Black Caucus." *Proceedings of the Academy of Political Science* 32: 34–50.

Beckman, Norman. 1985. "U.S. Budget Shifts Costs to States." *State Government News* 29: 12–13.

Bennett, Lerone Jr. 1963. "The Politics of the Outsider." *Negro Digest* 17: 5–8.

Bessette, Joseph M. 1994. *The Mild Voice of Reason: Deliberative Democracy and American National Government.* Chicago: University of Chicago Press.

Bobo, Lawrence and Franklin D. Gilliam Jr. 1990. "Race, Sociopolitical Participation, and Black Empowerment." *American Political Science Review* 84: 377–90.

Bowsher, Charles A. 1986. "Federal Cutbacks Strengthen State Role." *State Government News* 29: 18–21.

Bratton, Kathleen A. and Kerry L. Haynie. 1992. "Do Differences Matter? A Study of Race and Gender in State Legislatures." Presented at the annual meeting of the Southern Political Science Association, Atlanta.

——. 1999a. "Agenda Setting and Legislative Success in State Legislatures: The Effects of Gender and Race." *Journal of Politics* 61: 658–79.

——. 1999b. "The Representation of Interests Through Political Institutions: Race, Gender, and Committee Service." Binghamton University. Photocopy.

Browning, Rufus P., Dale R. Marshall, and David H. Tabb. 1984. *Protest Is Not Enough: The Struggle of Blacks and Hispanics for Equality in Urban Politics.* Berkeley: University of California Press.

Bullock, Charles. 1973. "Committee Transfers in the U.S. House of Representatives." *Journal of Politics* 35: 85–120.

——. 1975. "The Election of Blacks in the South: Preconditions and Consequences." *American Journal of Political Science* 19: 727–39.

——. 1981. "Congressional Voters and the Mobilization of a Black Electorate in the South." *Journal of Politics* 43: 662–82.

——. 1984. "Racial Crossover Voting and the Election of Black Public Officials." *Journal of Politics* 46: 238–51.

——. 1985. "U.S. Senate Committee Assignments: References, Motivations, and Success." *American Journal of Political Science* 29: 789–808.

Button, James W. 1989. *Blacks and Social Change: The Impact of the Civil Rights Movement in Southern Communities.* Princeton: Princeton University Press.

Button James and David Hedge. 1993. "Legislative Life in the 1990s: A Comparison of Black and White State Legislators." Presented at the annual meeting of the American Political Science Association, Washington, D.C.

——. 1996. "Legislative Life in the 1990s: A Comparison of Black And White State Legislators." *Legislative Studies Quarterly* 21: 199–218.

Button, James W. and Richard K. Scher. 1984. "The Election and Impact of Black Officials in the South." In Harrell R. Rodgers Jr., ed., *Public Policy and Social Institutions.* Greenwich, Conn.: JAI Press.

Cameron, Charles, David Epstein, and Sharon O'Halloran. 1996. "Do Majority-Minority Districts Maximize Substantive Black Representation in Congress?" *American Political Science Review* 90: 794–812.

Campbell, James D. and Joe Feagin. 1975. "Black Politics in the South: A Descriptive Analysis." *Journal of Politics* 37: 129–59.

Canon, David T. 1995. "Redistricting and the Congressional Black Caucus." *American Politics Quarterly* 23: 159–89.

———. 1999. *Race, Redistricting, and Representation: The Unintended Consequences of Black Majority Districts*. Chicago: University of Chicago Press.

Carroll, Susan J., ed. 1991. *Women, Black, and Hispanic State Elected Leaders*. New Brunswick, N.J.: Eagleton Institute of Politics.

Carsey, Thomas. 1995. "The Contextual Effect of Race on White Voter Behavior." *Journal of Politics* 57: 221–28.

Cavanagh, Thomas E. and Denise Stockton. 1983. *Black Elected Officials and Their Constituencies*. Washington, D.C.: Joint Center for Political and Economic Studies.

Citrin, Jack, Donald P. Green, and David O. Sears. 1990. "White Reactions to Black Candidates: When Does Race Matter?" *Public Opinion Quarterly* 54: 74–96.

Clapp, Charles L. 1963. *The Congressman: His Job As He Sees It*. Washington, D.C.: Brookings Institution.

Cobb, Roger W. and Charles D. Elder. 1983. *Participation in American Politics: The Dynamics of Agenda Building*. Baltimore: Johns Hopkins University Press.

Cole, Leonard A. 1976. *Black Power: A Comparative Study of Black and White Elected Officials*. Princeton: Princeton University Press.

Combs, Michael, John R. Hibbing, and Susan Welch. 1984. "Black Constituents and Congressional Roll Call Votes." *Western Political Quarterly* 37: 424–34.

Conyers, James E. and Walter Wallace. 1976. *Black Elected Officials*. New York: Russell Sage Foundation.

Cose, Ellis. 1997. "Joe Frazier for the Prosecution." In Cose, ed., *The Darden Dilemma*, 74–97. New York: HarperPerennial.

Dahl, Robert. 1956. *A Preface to Democratic Theory*. Chicago: University of Chicago Press.

———. 1961. *Who Governs? Democracy and Power in an American City*. New Haven: Yale University Press.

Davidson, Chandler. 1992. "The Voting Rights Act: A Brief History." In Grofman and Davidson, eds., *Controversies in Minority Voting*, 7–51.

Davidson, Chandler and Bernard Grofman, eds. 1994. *Quiet Revolution in the South: The Impact of the Voting Rights Act, 1965–1990*. Princeton, N.J.: Princeton University Press.

Davidson, Roger and Walter Oleszek. 1989. *Congress and Its Members*. 2d ed. Washington, D.C.: Congressional Quarterly Press.

Dawson, Michael C. 1994. *Behind the Mule: Race and Class in African-American Politics*. Princeton: Princeton University Press.

Denton, Van. 1962. "N.C. Blacks Stand to Make Big Political Gains." *Raleigh News and Observer*, October 4, 1A.

Dewart, Janet, ed. 1988. *The State of Black America*. New York: National Urban League.

——. 1989. *The State of Black America*. New York: National Urban League.

——. 1990. *The State of Black America*. New York: National Urban League.

——. 1991. *The State of Black America*. New York: National Urban League.

Di Lorenzo, Vincent. 1997. "Legislative Heart and Phase Transitions: An Exploratory Study of Congress and Minority Interests." *William and Mary Law Review* 38: 1729–1815.

Drake, St. Clair and Horace Cayton. 1945. *Black Metropolis*. Orlando, Fla.: Harcourt Brace Jovanovich.

Du Bois, W. E. B. 1961 (orig. 1903). *The Souls of Black Folk*. Greenwich, Conn.: Fawcett.

Dymally, Mervyn M., ed. 1971. *The Black Politician: His Struggle for Power*. Belmont, Calif.: Duxbury Press.

Erickson, Robert S. 1978. "Constituency Opinion and Congressional Behavior: A Reexamination of the Miller-Stokes Representation Data." *American Journal of Political Science* 22: 511–35.

Eulau, Heinz. 1962. "Bases of Authority in Legislative Bodies: A Comparative Analysis." *Administrative Science Quarterly* 7: 309–21.

——. 1967. "Changing Views of Representation." In Ithiel de Sola Pool, ed., *Contemporary Political Science: Toward Empirical Theory*. New York: McGraw-Hill.

——. 1985. "Committee Selection." In Gerhard Lowenberg, Samuel C. Patterson, and Malcolm E. Jewell, eds., *Handbook of Legislative Research*, 191–238. Cambridge: Harvard University Press.

Eulau, Heinz and Paul D. Karps. 1977. "The Puzzle of Representation: Specifying Components of Responsiveness." *Legislative Studies Quarterly* 2.3 (August): 233–54.

Fenno, Richard. 1966. *The Power of the Purse: Appropriations Politics in Congress*. Boston: Little, Brown.

——. 1973. *Congressmen in Committees*. Boston: Little, Brown.

——. 1978. *Home Style: House Members in Their Districts*. New York: Scott, Foresman.

Fiorina, Morris. 1989. *Congress: Keystone of the Washington Establishment*. 2d ed. New Haven: Yale University Press.

Francis, Wayne L. 1989. *The Legislative Committee Game: A Comparative Analysis of Fifty States*. Columbus: Ohio State University Press.

Frantzich, Stephen. 1979. "Who Makes Our Laws? The Legislative Effectiveness of Members of the U.S. Congress." *Legislative Studies Quarterly* 4: 409–28

Friedman, Sally. 1993. "Committee Advancement of Women and Blacks in Congress: A Test of the Responsible Legislator Thesis." *Women and Politics* 13: 27–52.

——. 1996. "House Committee Assignments of Women and Minority Newcomers, 1965–1994." *Legislative Studies Quarterly* 21: 73–82.

Gallie, W. B. 1962. "Essentially Contested Concepts." In Max Black, ed., *The Importance of Language*. Englewood Cliffs, N.J.: Prentice-Hall.

Gertzog, Irwin N. 1976. "The Routinization of Committee Assignments in the U.S. House of Representatives." *American Journal of Political Science* 20: 693–712.

———. 1984. *Congressional Women: Their Recruitment and Behavior.* New York: Praegar.

Giles, Michael W. and Melanie A. Buckner. 1993. "David Duke and Black Threat: An Old Hypothesis Revisited." *Journal of Politics* 55: 702–13.

Glaser, James. 1994. "Back to the Black Belt: Racial Environment and White Racial Attitudes in the South." *Journal of Politics* 56: 21–41.

Goodwin, George. 1970. *The Little Legislatures: Committees of Congress.* Boston: University of Massachusetts Press.

Grier, Kevin B. and Michael C. Munger. 1991. "Committee Assignments, Constituent Preferences, and Campaign Contributions." *Economic Inquiry* 29: 24–43.

Grofman, Bernard and Chandler Davidson. 1992. *Controversy in Minority Voting: The Voting Rights Act in Perspective.* Washington, D.C.: Brookings Institution.

Grofman, Bernard and Chandler Davidson, eds. 1977. *Controversies in Minority Voting: The Voting Rights Act in Perspective.* Washington, D.C.: Brookings Institution.

Grofman, Bernard and Lisa Handley. 1985. "The Impact of the Voting Rights Act on Black Representation in Southern State Legislatures." University of California, Irvine. Typescript.

———. 1989. "Minority Population Proportion and Black and Hispanic Congressional Success in the 1970s and 1980s." *American Politics Quarterly* 17: 436–45.

Grofman, Bernard, Robert Griffin, and Amihai Glazer. 1992. "The Effect of Black Population on Electing Democrats and Liberals to the House of Representatives." *Legislative Studies Quarterly* 17: 365–79.

Guinier, Lani. 1991. "The Triumph of Tokenism—the Voting Rights Act and the Theory of Black Electoral Success." *Michigan Law Review* 89: 1077–1154.

———. 1992. "Voting Rights and Democratic Theory: Where Do We Go from Here?" In Grofman and Davidson, eds., *Controversies in Minority Voting,* 283–92.

———. 1994. *The Tyranny of the Majority: Fundamental Fairness in Representative Democracy.* New York: Free Press.

Gurin, Patricia, Shirley Hatchett, and James S. Jackson. 1989. *Hope and Independence: Blacks' Response to Electoral and Party Politics.* New York: Russell Sage Foundation.

Gutman, Amy and Dennis Thompson. 1996. *Democracy and Disagreement.* Cambridge: Harvard University Press.

Hacker, Andrew. 1992. *Two Nations: Black and White, Separate, Hostile, Unequal.* New York: Scribner's.

Hall, Richard L. 1987. "Participation and Purpose in Committee Decision-Making." *American Political Science Review* 81: 105–28.

———. 1992. "Measuring Legislative Influence." *Legislative Studies Quarterly* 17: 205–31.

———. 1996. *Participation in Congress.* New Haven: Yale University Press.

Hall, Richard L. and Frank W. Wayman. 1990. "Buying Time: Moneyed Interests and the Mobilization of Bias in Congressional Committees." *American Political Science Review* 84: 797–820.

Hamilton, Charles V. 1977. "Deracialization: Examination of a Political Strategy." *First World* 1: 3–5.

Hamm, Keith E., Robert Harmel, and Robert Thompson. 1983. "Ethnic and Partisan Minorities in Two Southern Legislatures." *Legislative Studies Quarterly* 8: 177–89.

Haynie, Kerry L. 1999. "The Color of Their Skin or the Content of Their Behavior? Race and Perceptions of African American Officeholders." Rutgers University. Photocopy.

Hedge, David, James Button, and Mary Spear. 1996. "Accounting for the Quality of Black Legislative Life: The View from the States." *American Journal of Political Science* 40: 82–98.

Hedge, David M., James W. Button, and Richard K. Scher. 1992. "Black Legislative Leadership in the 1990s: A View from the States." Presented at the annual meeting of the American Political Science Association, Chicago.

Hedlund, Ronald. 1989. "Entering the Committee System: State Committee Assignments." *Western Political Quarterly* 42: 597–625.

———. 1992. "Accommodating Members Requests in Committee Assignments: Individual-Level Explanations." In Moncrief and Thompson, eds., *Changing Patterns in State Legislative Careers*, 149–74.

Hedlund, Ronald and Diane Powers. 1987. "Constancy of Committee Membership in 16 States: 1971–86." Paper presented at the annual meeting of the Midwest Political Science Association, Cincinnati, Ohio.

Herring, Mary. 1990. "Legislative Responsiveness to Black Constituents in Three Deep South States." *Journal of Politics* 52: 740–58.

Hibbing, John R. 1991. *Congressional Careers: Contours of Life in the U.S. House of Representatives.* Chapel Hill: University of North Carolina Press.

———. 1993. "Careerism in Congress." In Lawrence C. Dodd and Bruce I. Oppenheimer. eds., *Congress Reconsidered*, 67–90. Washington, D.C.: Congressional Quarterly Press.

Huitt, Ralph K. 1957. "The Morese Committee Assignment Controversy: A Study in Senate Norms." *American Political Science Review* 51: 313–29.

———. 1961. "The Outsider in the Senate." *American Political Science Review* 55: 566–75.

Ippolito, Dennis S., William S. Donaldson, and Lewis Bowman. 1968. "Political Orientations Among Negroes and Whites." In Norval D. Glenn and Charles M. Bojean, eds., *Blacks in the United States*, 105–13. San Francisco: Chandler.

Jacobson, Gary C. 1992. *The Politics of Congressional Elections.* New York: Harper-Collins.

Jewell, Malcom E. 1969. *The State Legislature.* New York: Random House.

——. 1982. *Representation in State Legislatures.* Lexington, Ky.: University of Kentucky Press.

——. 1983. "Legislator-Constituent Relations and the Representative Process." *Legislative Studies Quarterly* 13: 303–37.

Joint Center for Political and Economic Studies. 1998. *Black Elected Officials.* Washington, D.C.: Joint Center for Political and Economic Studies.

Karnig, Albert and Susan Welch. 1980. *Black Representation and Urban Policy.* Chicago: University of Chicago Press.

Keech, William R. 1968. *The Impact of Negro Voting: The Role of the Vote in the Quest for Equality.* Chicago: Rand McNally.

Keefe, William J. and Morris S. Ogul. 1993. *The American Legislative Process.* Englewood Cliffs, N.J.: Prentice-Hall.

Key, V. O. 1949. *Southern Politics: In State and Nation.* New York: Knopf.

Kinder, Donald R. 1986. "The Continuing American Dilemma: White Resistance to Racial Change Forty Years After Myrdal." *Journal of Social Issues* 42: 151–72.

Kinder, Donald and David O. Sears. 1981. "Prejudice and Politics: Symbolic Racism Versus Racial Threats to the Good Life." *Journal of Personality and Social Psychology* 40: 414–31.

King, Gary. 1988. "Statistical Models for Political Science Event Counts: Bias in Conventional Procedures and Evidence for the Exponential Poisson Regression Model." *American Journal of Political Science* 32: 838–63.

——. 1989. *Unifying Political Methodology.* New York: Cambridge University Press.

Kingdon, John W. 1981. *Congressmen's Voting Decisions.* 2d ed. New York: Harper and Row.

——. 1984. *Agendas, Alternatives, and Public Policies.* Boston: Little, Brown.

——. 1989. *Congressmen's Voting Decisions.* 3d ed. Ann Arbor: University of Michigan Press.

Kochack, K. D., J. D. Maurer, and H. M. Rosenberg. 1994. "Why Did Black Life Expectancy Decline from 1984 Through 1989 in the United States?" *American Journal of Public Health* 84: 938–44.

Lawson, Stephen F. 1985. *In Pursuit of Power: Southern and Electoral Politics, 1965–1982.* New York: Columbia University Press.

Lewis, J. A. and William Schneider. 1983. "Black Voting, Bloc Voting, and the Democrats." *Public Opinion* 6: 12–15.

Lieberman, Robert C. 1993. "The Structural Politics of Race: Toward a New Approach to the Study of Race and Politics." Presented at the annual meeting of the American Political Science Association, Chicago.

——. 1995. "Race and the Organization of Welfare Policy." In Paul E. Peterson, ed., *Classifying by Race,* 156–87. Princeton: Princeton University Press.

Lublin, David I. 1997. *The Paradox of Representation: Racial Gerrymander and Minority Interests in Congress.* Princeton: Princeton University Press.

Manin, Bernard. 1997. *The Principles of Representative Government*. Cambridge: Cambridge University Press.

Mansbridge, Jane. 1999. "Should Blacks Represent Blacks and Women Represent Women? A Contingent 'Yes.'" *Journal of Politics* 61: 628–57.

Mahtesian, Charles. 1996. "Best and Dimmest." *Governing* 9.5: 24–28.

Massey, Douglas S. and Nancy A. Denton. 1993. *American Apartheid: Segregation and the Making of the Underclass*. Cambridge: Harvard University Press.

Masters, Nicholas. 1961. "Committee Assignments in the House of Representatives." *American Political Science Review* 55: 345–57.

Matthews, Donald R. 1960. *U.S. Senators and Their World*. New York: Vintage.

Mayhew, David R. 1974. *Congress: The Electoral Connection*. New Haven: Yale University Press.

McClain, Paula D. 1990. "Agenda Setting, Public Policy, and Minority Group Influence: An Introduction." *Policy Studies Review* 9: 263–72.

McCormick, Joseph P. II. 1989. "Black Tuesday and the Politics of Deracialization." Paper presented at a symposium, "Blacks in the November '89 Elections: What Is Changing?" Sponsored by the Joint Center for Political Studies, Washington, D.C., December 1989.

McCormick, Joseph P. II and Charles E. Jones. 1993. "The Conceptualization of Deracialization: Thinking Through the Dilemma." In Persons, ed., *Dilemmas of Black Politics*, 66–84.

McGriggs, Lee Augustus. 1977. *Black Legislative Politics in Illinois: A Theoretical and Structural Analysis*. Washington, D.C.: University Press of America.

Meyer, Katherine. 1980. "Legislative Influence: Toward Theory Development Through Causal Analysis." *Legislative Studies Quarterly* 4: 563–85.

Miller, Cheryl M. 1990. "Agenda-Setting by State Legislative Black Caucuses: Policy Priorities and Factors of Success." *Policy Studies Review* 9: 339–54.

Miller, Warren E. and Donald E. Stokes. 1963. "Constituency Influence in Congress." *American Political Science Review* 57: 45–56.

Moncrief, Gary F. and Joel A. Thompson, eds. 1992. *Changing Patterns in State Legislative Careers*. Ann Arbor: University of Michigan Press.

Morris, Aldon M. 1984. *The Origin of the Civil Rights Movement: Black Communities Organizing for Change*. New York: Free Press.

Moynihan, Daniel Patrick. 1965 (March). *The Negro Family*. Washington, D.C.: Office of Policy Planning and Research, U.S. Department of Labor.

Munger, Michael C. 1988. "Allocation of Desirable Committee Assignments: Extended Queues Versus Committee Expansion." *American Journal of Political Science* 32: 317–44.

Nathan, Richard P. and Fred C. Doolittle. 1987. "The Evolution of Federal Aid." In Nathan and Doolittle, eds., *Reagan and the States*, 22–43. Princeton: Princeton University Press.

National Center for Health Statistics. 1994. *Health in the United States 1993.* Hyattsville, Md.: U.S. Department of Health and Human Services.

Nelson, Albert J. 1991. *Emerging Influentials in State Legislatures: Women, Black, and Hispanics.* New York: Praeger.

North Carolina Center for Public Policy Research (NCCPPR). 1978. *Article II: A Guide to the North Carolina Legislature.* Raleigh: NCCPPR.

Olson, David M. and Cynthia T. Nonidez. 1972. "Measures of Legislative Performance in the U.S. House of Representatives." *Midwest Journal of Political Science* 16: 269–77.

Perry, Robert T. 1976. *Black Legislators.* San Francisco: R and E Research Associates.

Persons, Georgia A., ed. 1993. *Dilemmas of Black Politics: Issues of Leadership and Strategy.* New York: HarperCollins.

Peterson, Paul E. 1995. *The Price of Federalism.* Washington, D.C.: Brookings Institution.

Pettigrew, Thomas F. 1976. "Black Mayoral Campaigns." In H. J. Bryce, ed., *Urban Governance and Minorities,* 14–29. New York: Praeger.

Pinderhughes, Dianne. 1987. *Race and Ethnicity in Chicago Politics.* Urbana: University of Illinois Press.

Pitkin, Hanna F. 1967. *The Concept of Representation.* Berkeley: University of California Press.

Reeves, Keith. 1997. *Voting Hopes and Fears: White Voters, Black Candidates, and Racial Politics in America.* New York: Oxford University Press.

Rhode, David W. and Kenneth A. Shepsle. 1973. "Democratic Committee Assignments in the House of Representatives: Strategic Aspects of a Social Choice Process." *American Political Science Review* 67: 889–905.

Rogers, W. H. 1993. "Regression Standard Errors in Clustered Samples." *Stata Technical Bulletin* 13: 19–23.

Rosenthal, Alan. 1974. *Legislative Performance in the States: Exploration of Committee Behavior.* New York: Free Press.

———. 1981. *Legislative Life: Process and Performance in the States.* New York: Harper and Row.

Rosenthal, Alan. 1990. *Governors and Legislatures: Contending Powers.* Washington, D.C.: CQ Press.

Sapiro, Virginia. 1981. "Research Frontier Essay: When Are Interests Interesting the Problem of Political Representation of Women?" *American Political Science Review* 75: 701–16.

Sargent, Jocelyn. 1991. "Black Interests and Representation." Paper presented at the annual meeting of the American Political Science Association, Washington, D.C.

Schattschneider, E. E. 1960. *The Semi-Sovereign People.* New York: Holt, Rinehart, and Winston.

Schuman, Howard, Charlotte Steeh, and L. Bobo. 1985. *Racial Attitudes in America: Trends and Interpretations.* Cambridge: Harvard University Press.

Sears, David O., Jack Citrin, and R. Kosterman. 1987. "Jesse Jackson and the Southern White Electorate in 1984." In L. Moreland, R. Steed, and T. Baker, eds., *Blacks in Southern Politics,* 209–25. New York: Praeger.

Shepsle, Kenneth A. 1975. "Congressional Committee Assignments: An Optimization Model with Institutional Constraints." *Public Choice* 21: 55–78.

———. 1978. *The Giant Jigsaw Puzzle: Democratic Committee Assignments in the Modern House.* Chicago: University of Chicago Press.

———. 1988. "Representation and Governance: The Great Trade-off." *Political Science Quarterly* 103: 461–83.

Sigelman, Carol K., Lee Sigelman, Barbara J. Walkosz, and Michael Nitz. 1995. "Black Candidates, White Voters: Understanding Racial Bias in Political Perceptions." *American Journal of Political Science* 39: 243–65.

Sinclair, Barbara. 1981. "Agenda and Alignment Change: The House of Representatives, 1925–1978." In Lawrence C. Dodd and Bruce I. Oppenheimer, eds., *Congress Reconsidered,* 291–314. Washington, D.C.: Congressional Quarterly Press.

Skocpol, Theda. 1991. "Targeting Within Universalism: Politically Viable Politics to Combat Poverty in the United States." In Christopher Jencks and Paul E. Peterson, eds., *The Urban Underclass.* Washington, D.C.: Brookings Institution.

Smith, Robert C. 1990. "The Death of Black Politics?" Presented at the annual meeting of the National Conference of Black Political Scientists, Atlanta.

———. 1995. *Racism in the Post-Civil Rights Era: Now You See it, Now You Don't.* Albany: State University of New York Press.

———. 1996. *We Have No Leaders: African Americans in the Post-Civil Rights Era.* Albany: State University of New York Press.

Smith, Steven S. and Christopher J. Deering. 1984. *Committees in Congress.* Washington, D.C.: Congressional Quarterly Press.

———. *Committees in Congress.* 2d ed. Washington, D.C.: CQ Press.

Sonenshein. Raphael J. 1993. *Politics in Black and White: Race and Power in Los Angeles.* Princeton: Princeton University Press.

Stewart, Charles, III. 1992. "Committee Hierarchies in the Modernizing House, 1875–1947." *American Journal of Political Science* 36: 835–56.

Stone, Walter. 1979. "Measuring Constituency-Representative Linkages: Problems and Prospects." *Legislative Studies Quarterly* 4: 623–39.

Swain, Carol M. 1993. *Black Faces, Black Interests: The Representation of African Americans in Congress.* Cambridge: Harvard University Press.

Swinter, David H. 1992. "The Economic State of African Americans: Limited Ownership and Persistent Inequality." In Tidwell, ed., *The State of Black America, 1992,* 61–117.

Tate, Katherine. 1993. *From Protest to Politics: The New Black Voters in American Elections.* Cambridge: Harvard University Press.

Terkildsen, Nadia. 1993. "When White Voters Evaluate Black Candidates: The Processing Implications of Candidate Skin Color, Prejudice, and Self-Monitoring." *American Journal of Political Science* 37: 1032–53.

Thernstrom, Abigail. 1987. *Whose Votes Count? Affirmative Action and Minority Voting Rights.* Cambridge: Harvard University Press.

Thernstrom. Stephan and Abigail Thernstrom. 1997. *America in Black and White—One Nation Indivisible: Race in Modern America.* New York: Simon and Schuster.

Thomas, Sue. 1991. "The Impact of Women on State Legislative Policies." *Journal of Politics* 53: 958–76.

——. 1994. *How Women Legislate.* New York: Oxford University Press.

Tidwell, Billy J., ed. 1992. *The State of Black America, 1992.* New York: National Urban League.

U.S. Department of Commerce. Bureau of the Census. 1991. *Statistical Abstract of the United States.* Washington, D.C.: Department of Commerce.

Wahlke, John C., Heinz Eulau, William Buchanan, and Leroy C. Ferguson. 1962. *The Legislative System: Exploration in Legislative Behavior.* New York: John Wiley.

Walker, Jack L. 1977. "Setting the Agenda in the U.S. Senate: A Theory of Problem Selection." *British Journal of Politics* 7: 423–45.

Walters, Ronald. 1992. "The Two Political Traditions: Black Politics in the 1990s." *National Political Science Review* 3: 198–207.

Walton, Hanes, Jr. and Leslie Burl McLemore. 1970. "A Portrait of Black Political Styles." *Black Politician* 2: 9–13.

Weissert, Carol S. 1989. "Determinants and Dynamics of Perceived Legislative Effectiveness in the North Carolina State Legislature, 1977–1987." Ph.D. diss., University of North Carolina at Chapel Hill.

——. 1991. "Issue Salience and State Legislative Effectiveness." *Legislative Studies Quarterly* 16: 509–20.

Whitby, Kenny J. 1985. "Voting Behavior of Southern Congressmen: The Interaction of Race and Urbanization." *Legislative Studies Quarterly* 10: 505–17.

——. 1987. "Measuring Congressional Responsiveness to the Policy Interests of Constituents." *Social Science Quarterly* 68: 367–77.

——. 1997. *The Color of Representation: Congressional Behavior and Black Interests.* Ann Arbor: University of Michigan Press.

Whitby, Kenny J. and Franklin D. Gilliam Jr. 1991. "A Longitudinal Analysis of Competing Explanations for the Transformation of Southern Congressional Politics." *Journal of Politics* 53: 504–18.

White, H. 1980. "A Heteroskedasticity-consistent Covariance Estimator and a Direct Test for Heteroskedasticity." *Econometrica* 48: 817–30.

White, William S. 1956. *Citadel: The Story of the U.S. Senate.* New York: Harper.

Wilson, James. 1960. "Two Negro Politicians: An Interpretation." *Midwest Journal of Political Science* 4: 144–62.

Wilson, William J. 1987. *The Truly Disadvantaged: The Inner City, the Underclass, and Public Policy.* Chicago: University of Chicago Press.

———. 1990. "Race-Neutral Programs and the Democratic Coalition." *The American Prospect* 1 (Spring): 74–81.

Wolfinger, Raymond. 1974. *The Politics of Progress.* Englewood Cliffs, N.J.: Prentice-Hall.

INDEX

African American interests. *See* black
  interests
African Americans: "black utility
  heuristic" and, 18, 106; as cohesive
  and consistent political subgroup,
  19, 42; progress for, in some areas,
  47; voters' views of, as candidates,
  93. *See also* black interests
African American state legislators:
  broadening of agendas, 62;
  commonality-type, 48; dearth of
  scholarly literature on, 2–3;
  dilemma faced by, 4–6; expansion of
  presence on nonblack-interest
  committees, 54; impact of
  redistricting decisions, 34;
  importance to constituencies and
  black interests, 15–16, 34; increase in
  numbers of, 2, 15; legislative
  effectiveness of, 94–95; as legislative
  subgroup, 49; numbers and

percentages by state/year, 11 (*table*);
  political incorporation, 65–68, 69
  (*table*), 70 (*table*), 70; as primary
  advocates for black interests, 27–28;
  as "race men/women" and "race
  representatives," 4, 9, 16–17, 31, 34, 61,
  108, 113; as "responsible legislators"
  with "balancing perspective," 9–11,
  34, 62, 106, 109, 113; "significant
  numbers" question, 129n5. *See also*
  descriptive representation; race as
  factor in peer evaluations
American states. *See* Arkansas; Illinois;
  Maryland; New Jersey; North
  Carolina; and states
Anderson, Elijah, 4, 7, 107
appropriations committees, 100, 101
  (*table*), 102 (*table*)
Arkansas: African American state
  legislators, numbers and
  percentages by year, 11 (*table*);

study data. *See* data sources,
conceptualizations, and methods
"substantive" bill introductions, 123*n*12
substantive representation, 16, 35
Supreme Court decisions, 34
Swain, Carol, 35, 108
Swinter, David H., 20

Tabb, David H., 64, 66, 70–71, 89, 90,
107
tax capacity, 82–83, 84 (*table*), 85
(*table*), 87 (*table*), 88 (*table*)
Thomas, Sue, 12

unemployment rates, black and
nonblack, 20 (*table*)

"universal" programs, 122*n*11
urbanness, 29, 32 (*table*)

voter registration and turnout, 17, 47,
65, 107
Voting Rights Act of 1965, 1, 3–4, 17, 63

Walker, Jack L., 25
Weissert, Carol S., 94, 98
welfare issues, 18, 26, 30, 32–33 (*table*),
77–79, 79 (*table*), 80 (*table*), 81
(*table*)
Whitby, Kenny J., 18–19, 36
Wilson, William Julius, 10
women legislators, 9, 29, 30, 32–33
(*table*), 124*n*15, 128*n*1

Power, Conflict, and Democracy:
American Politics Into the Twenty-first Century